Important Note: In a formal book, it would be essential to cite all external resources, references, and quotes to maintain academic integrity and avoid plagiarism. However, in this book, the information provided is not directly lifted from external sources but is general knowledge within the field of AI. Therefore, an index or citations may not be strictly necessary for this specific chapter content.

Since ChatGPT generated all the content and none of it was sourced from specific, citable materials, a traditional bibliography isn't necessary in this context. All the information provided is the result of synthesized data programmed into ChatGPT's training model, so you could say that the material reflects general knowledge up to its last training cut-off in September 2021.

For academic or highly fact-based works, it's usually critical to cite sources, but since the text provided by ChatGPT was generated based on a large corpus of data that it was trained on, and not direct citations from copyrighted material, there are no specific sources to cite.

Copyright

Preface

The title "**>run, When to Get in the Way**" is more than just an eye-catching phrase. It encapsulates the complex dilemma at the heart of this book: when should humans step in and take control in a world increasingly governed by Artificial Intelligence? In computer programming, a "run" command initiates a series of automated operations. But when those operations have far-reaching ethical, social, and personal implications, merely initiating a "run" command is insufficient. This book aims to help you know when to "run" with technological advancements and when to step in and assert human values.

Ironically, the very subject of this book—the complex interplay between humans and AI—also underpins its creation. That's right; your eyes aren't deceiving you. I, Kenyon Ross, orchestrated the vision for this book, but the elaborate tapestry of words that unfolds across these pages is largely woven by an AI model known as GPT-4.

In today's rapidly evolving landscape, AI's tendrils reach into almost every aspect of life. As someone plagued by the challenges of focus and attention—traits often connected with ADD—I find the process of writing to be a Herculean task. Yet, here we are, on the cusp of a book that wouldn't exist without AI's assistance, providing a layer of irony so thick you could cut it with a knife.

To the traditional authors who painstakingly craft every sentence, I extend my deepest respect. Your labor of love sets the gold standard for what writing can be. Ironically, while you might spend years on your craft, I've wrapped up the first five chapters of this book in a single morning. By Monday, I expect this book to be typeset and listed on Amazon. You can't make this stuff up.

But who, then, owns this creation? Is it the AI model spitting out text in response to my prompts, or is it me, directing the narrative, raising questions, and tying together loose ends? We find ourselves in a nebulous space where human ingenuity meets mechanical prowess, and the lines of authorship blur.

The chapters that unfold here aim to cut through the ambiguity surrounding AI, from its applications in healthcare and the workplace to its ethical considerations and impact on the arts. Each chapter seeks to explore a unique facet of AI's integration into human life. The text aims to serve as both a practical guide and a philosophical inquiry into our coexistence with artificial intelligence.

As you delve deeper into these pages, you'll find that the book itself serves as an example of what it argues. It's a hybrid product of human intuition and machine capability, urging you to ponder the complexities this partnership presents. In these pages, you'll encounter the very real challenges that come with AI's proliferation. We'll probe the ethical questions surrounding machine-generated art, delve into the military's use of autonomous weaponry, and examine how AI could reshape our educational systems. We'll even take a close look at how AI is poised to redefine our understanding of healthcare, transforming patient care but also raising questions about empathy and human connection.

You may find yourself asking, "Is AI a boon or a bane?" The answer is far from straightforward, and this book doesn't shy away from examining the gray areas. It's crucial that we, as a society, figure out our stance before we reach a point of no return, before the ">run" command is irrevocably initiated, leaving us spectators in our own lives.

I must acknowledge the elephant in the room: can this book, a collaboration between man and machine, be considered a credible source? This very project aims to shake the grounds of traditional authorship, and I invite you, the reader, to form your own opinion. Does the blend of machine-compiled data and human-directed flow result in a lesser product? Or does it introduce a fresh perspective, a new way of dissecting complex topics?

If nothing else, this book serves as a living testament to the evolving nature of creation and collaboration in the 21st century. As you turn these pages, I urge you to grapple not just with the information presented but also with the meta questions about the book's own existence. This duality—both as an exploration and an example of AI's societal impact—aims to enrich your understanding and challenge your preconceptions.

I hope this book gives you the tools and perspectives to engage more deeply with the world of AI, to understand when to embrace its possibilities and when tc exert human judgment—in essence, when to ">run" and when to get in the way. And so, with an open mind and perhaps a touch of skepticism, let's embark on this journey together.

Table of Contents

Chapter 1: Models of Imperfection

The Mirage of Perfection

In a world obsessed with precision and performance, the introduction of Artificial Intelligence (AI) feels like a logical next step. We have smartphones that predict what we want to type next, virtual assistants that play our favorite songs on command, and even self-driving cars inching ever closer to commercial reality. It's almost as if we're building toward some utopia where human error is a thing of the past—a mirage of perfection conjured by digital intelligence.

But let's snap back to reality. These digital phenomena are not birthed from some ethereal realm of flawlessness. They are the products of algorithms, data, and most importantly, human ingenuity and error. The mathematical models underpinning AI systems are often mistaken for impartial godsends. In truth, they are far from it. These models carry the same baggage of imperfection and bias that their human creators do, only more obscurely.

Algorithms and Data: A Symbiotic Relationship

An algorithm is essentially a set of rules to be followed in problem-solving operations, and in the world of AI, it operates on data. Think of it as a recipe. A recipe alone can't make a dish; you need ingredients. In AI, algorithms are the recipes and data are the ingredients. Together, they produce results, which can be as delightful as a well-made dish or as disastrous as a cooking fiasco.

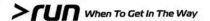

Data serves as the fuel for algorithms, but it's essential to understand that data is never inherently neutral. Every piece of information is a slice of a larger context, shaped by human understanding and societal norms. When a dataset is riddled with systemic inequalities, the algorithm trained on it not only learns those inequalities but often amplifies them.

Filling in the Gaps: The AI Dilemma

The AI systems of today are not self-aware entities; they don't possess understanding or consciousness. They are robust pattern recognition systems. They can analyze more data in a minute than a human can in a lifetime. But their expertise comes with an array of limitations. The gaps in their learning models make them prone to bizarre and sometimes dangerous mistakes, errors that a human expert would not make. For instance, an AI model trained to identify animals might label a clear picture of a cat as a dog if it hasn't been adequately trained on that particular breed of cat.

AI's limitations are not just about wrong categorizations or harmless blunders. They can have severe real-world implications. AI models are now used in critical areas like healthcare for diagnosis, in law enforcement for predictive policing, and even in autonomous vehicles. When an AI model misdiagnoses a medical condition or falsely identifies someone as a criminal risk, the stakes are high.

When To Get In the Way

The conundrum we face is how much we should intervene in AI's decision-making process. Should we always "get out of the way" and allow the machine to make decisions for us, trusting in its vast data analysis capabilities? Or are there situations where human oversight is not only beneficial but essential – when should we get in the way? It's easy to imagine scenarios in which allowing AI to operate independently could result in better outcomes, especially in data-heavy fields like finance or logistics. But it's equally simple to envisage high-stakes settings like healthcare or law enforcement where machine error could cost lives or compromise justice.

—

Balancing machine autonomy and human intervention is a tightrope walk, and the winds of technological change only make it more precarious. It's not just about how accurately a machine can diagnose a disease or predict a stock market trend; it's about the ethical, social, and philosophical implications of letting a non-human entity make decisions that affect human lives. The question isn't just about machine capabilities; it's also about human values, ethical considerations, and the kind of society we want to build.

When we take a step back, it's clear that AI, in its current state, is not an infallible oracle but a tool—one that is incredibly powerful but also deeply flawed. Just like any tool, its effectiveness is determined by the skill and wisdom with which it is used. As we navigate this complex relationship with AI, our challenge is to discern when to step aside and when to intervene, understanding that sometimes the most rational thing to do is to get in the way.

The Paradox of Terminology

As we delve deeper into the world of artificial intelligence, we're often confronted by terms that borrow from human cognition—words like 'learning,' 'understanding,' and even 'thinking.' These terms present a peculiar paradox. On the one hand, they make AI systems more relatable, almost as if we're talking about a new form of life. On the other hand, they can be profoundly misleading.

AI doesn't 'learn' in the way humans do. There's no awareness, no consciousness, no subjective experience behind the algorithms. When machine learning models 'learn,' they are adjusting mathematical weights in a complex multi-dimensional space based on the error rates of their predictions. Sounds less like learning and more like fine-tuning, doesn't it?

Moreover, the term 'thinking' is a gross overstatement for what AI does. Human thought is a complex interplay of consciousness, emotions, abstract reasoning, and creativity. Machines are far from achieving this level of sophistication. So, why do we use such terminology? One reason might be anthropomorphism, our tendency to attribute human traits to non-human entities. It's easier to say a machine 'learns' or 'thinks,' as it helps us relate to what would otherwise be a faceless algorithm. But this ease comes at a cost: the risk of misunderstanding what these systems can and cannot do.

Understanding the limits of AI's 'cognition' helps us make more informed decisions about its applications and implications. It tempers our expectations and guides us in framing more realistic questions about the technology's capabilities and limitations. For example, asking whether an AI model can 'understand' human emotions is misleading. A more accurate question would be: can this model accurately classify textual data into categories that we interpret as emotional states? By being precise in our terminology, we reduce the risk of attributing capabilities to AI that it doesn't possess, guiding us towards a more grounded and realistic approach to integrating it into our lives.

Understanding the nuances of AI terminology is not just a semantic exercise; it has practical implications. Consider the legal and ethical frameworks that are still evolving around AI. If we think of an AI system as 'understanding' or 'thinking,' we might be tempted to assign it a level of agency or responsibility that it doesn't possess. This misunderstanding could lead to misplaced accountability in cases where AI systems make decisions that have legal or ethical ramifications.

Furthermore, the paradox of terminology becomes more poignant when we look at AI's role in sensitive applications like healthcare or criminal justice. In these fields, a machine's 'decision' can have life-altering consequences. Therefore, understanding that a machine doesn't 'decide' in the way a human does is crucial. It doesn't weigh moral or ethical considerations; it follows the pattern it has 'learned' from its training data. Understanding this helps us in putting the right safety mechanisms in place—like human oversight, ethical guidelines, and fail-safes.

—

Finally, clarifying the terminology we use to describe AI's capabilities allows us to navigate the moral and philosophical terrain more skillfully. Does a machine that 'learns' have rights? Can a machine that 'thinks' be conscious? These questions might sound absurd to some, but they're being discussed in academic and ethical circles. The consensus, for now, is that machines don't possess the qualities these terms describe in humans—consciousness, subjective experience, ethical reasoning. Therefore, they don't have rights, nor can they bear responsibilities. But it's essential to keep revisiting these questions as AI technology evolves, and being clear about the terms we use is a crucial first step in that direction.

So, the next time you hear about an AI system 'learning,' 'thinking,' or 'understanding,' take a moment to consider what those words genuinely mean in the context of machine intelligence. Clarifying our language can help us clarify our thinking, leading us to interact with AI technology in a way that is both more ethical and more effective.

Navigating the world of artificial intelligence requires not just technological understanding but also philosophical discernment. The language we use to describe these machines ultimately shapes our relationship with them, influencing public policy, legal frameworks, and societal attitudes. Therefore, it's crucial to recognize the limitations and opportunities inherent in the terminology we use.

For example, consider the word 'autonomous' when describing self-driving cars or drones. The term implies a level of independence and self-governance that these machines simply do not possess. In reality, they operate based on a set of rules and algorithms set by human programmers. Misunderstanding this term can lead to unrealistic expectations and misplaced trust. If we think of these machines as 'autonomous' in the same way we think of adult humans as autonomous, we risk overlooking the fact that they are ultimately under human control and can be prone to errors of various kinds.

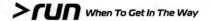

The stakes are not merely academic. For instance, in the legal realm, defining the terms clearly is fundamental. If an autonomous vehicle is involved in an accident, is it the fault of the 'autonomous' vehicle, or does liability fall squarely on the shoulders of the humans who programmed it? Our understanding of these terms can directly influence legal proceedings and the subsequent development of laws surrounding AI technology.

Similarly, AI in healthcare is often described as 'assistive' technology. What do we mean by 'assistive'? Are these systems merely tools in the hands of medical professionals, or are they partners in diagnosis and treatment? Clarifying this can have substantial implications for medical practice and malpractice law.

In the world of AI ethics, we often hear the term 'algorithmic bias.' What do we mean by 'bias'? Is it the same as human bias, which is often rooted in societal prejudices, or is it something fundamentally different, arising from flawed data or skewed algorithms? Addressing the issue starts with defining the problem accurately.

To summarize, the paradox of terminology in AI is not a trivial matter. It shapes our collective understanding of what these powerful tools can and cannot do. It informs ethical considerations, influences legal frameworks, and impacts societal trust in these technologies. As we continue to integrate AI into various aspects of our lives, we must strive for clarity and precision in our language, ensuring that our words accurately reflect the capabilities and limitations of these extraordinary machines.

By focusing on the terms we use, we can ensure more effective and ethical interactions with AI, recognizing both its incredible potential and its inherent limitations. Only through clear language can we hope to navigate the complex ethical and societal landscapes that AI has already begun to transform.

Certainly! Let's delve deeper into the Ethics of AI for Chapter 2. We'll begin by elaborating on the importance of ethics in AI and discuss the many dimensions of ethical AI.

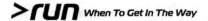

Chapter 2: The Ethics of AI

Introduction: The Moral Quandary

Artificial intelligence is rapidly transforming the landscape of various industries, from healthcare to finance, education to transportation. But with great power comes great responsibility. As AI systems become more intelligent and autonomous, the question of ethics becomes increasingly pertinent. The challenge is not just to develop AI that is effective but also ethical, ensuring that it serves humanity while respecting societal norms and individual rights.

Why Ethics Matter in AI

AI systems can process large sets of data at incredible speeds, but they lack the moral reasoning that human beings have. It's easy to think that algorithms are neutral, crunching numbers without any sense of right or wrong. However, the reality is far more complex. These algorithms are created by humans, trained on data generated by humans, and ultimately deployed in environments that directly affect humans. Thus, the ethical dimensions of AI are not merely an add-on but a fundamental aspect that shapes its impact on society.

For instance, consider an AI system used in criminal justice for risk assessment. If the data used to train this system includes historical biases, the AI could inadvertently exacerbate existing inequalities, disproportionately affecting minority communities. Without careful ethical considerations, we risk deploying AI systems that perpetuate or even amplify societal injustices.

Fairness and Bias

One of the most talked-about ethical concerns in AI is the issue of fairness and bias. How do we ensure that AI algorithms are fair to all individuals, regardless of their race, gender, or socioeconomic status? And how do we prevent biases in training data from infiltrating the AI models?

It's crucial to scrutinize the data used in training AI models. If the dataset contains biases, the AI system will learn those biases, perpetuating and perhaps even amplifying them. What if for example, a study found that a healthcare algorithm widely used in the United States was less likely to refer certain race of pat ents to programs that aim to improve care for patients with complex medical needs, despite being equally sick as different race. The algo ithm's bias would have an unintended consequence of the data it was trained on, which would have underlying racial biases.

Accountability and Transparency

Another core tenet of ethical AI is accountability. As AI systems increasingly make decisions that impact human lives, it's crucial to identify who or what is accountable for those decisions. In many instances, there's a lack of clarity about this. If an AI system misdiagnoses a patient, who is responsible—the developers of the algorithm, the medical professionals who relied on it, or the hospital that deployed it?

This question becomes more complex as AI systems evolve toward greater autonomy. In the case of self-driving cars, for instance, the car's AI system decides how to navigate through traffic, obey speed limits, and avoid obstacles. If a self-driving car were to cause an accident, determining accountability could become a legal and ethical quagmire. Therefore, it is crucial to establish well-defined guidelines for accountability in AI to safeguard individual rights and societal values.

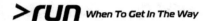 *When To Get In The Way*

Transparency is closely related to accountability. It refers to the idea that the inner workings of an AI system should be understandable to people who use it or are affected by it. However, many of today's machine learning algorithms, particularly deep learning models, are notoriously hard to interpret. They function like "black boxes," where it's difficult to pinpoint how exactly they arrive at a particular decision.

The need for transparency also extends to data. As we have noted earlier, biased, or flawed data can lead to skewed outcomes. Openly discussing the sources and types of data used can be a step towards more ethical AI. Organizations should ideally disclose how they collect, store, and process data, ensuring that it meets ethical standards.

The Moral Machine

Human beings have pondered moral dilemmas for centuries, discussing complex scenarios where ethical considerations clash. In the world of AI, these dilemmas often materialize quite literally. Take, for example, the well-known "trolley problem. " a thought experiment in ethics. Imagine a self-driving car faced with an impossible choice: to swerve and hit a pedestrian or stay the course and collide with a vehicle, potentially harming its passengers. How should the car's AI make this moral decision?

While this example may seem extreme, it illustrates the types of decisions AI systems may have to make as they become more integrated into our lives. Programming ethics into a machine is not straightforward, and what's considered "moral" can vary widely depending on cultural, societal, or individual beliefs.

The concept of a "Moral Machine" is not just a theoretical idea but a very real challenge for AI developers. There have been initiatives to crowdsource public opinion on ethical dilemmas that self-driving cars might face, aiming to integrate a form of "collective intelligence" into the algorithms. Such approaches, while innovative, also come with their own set of ethical questions, such as whose morality is being represented and who gets to decide what is "right" or "wrong."

Ethical Frameworks for AI Development

To tackle these questions and dilemmas, various ethical frameworks have been proposed, often grounded in long-standing theories of ethics, such as utilitarianism or deontological ethics. Utilitarian approaches aim for the "greatest good for the greatest number," focusing on outcomes rather than actions. In contrast, deontological ethics centers on the morality of the action itself, regardless of the result.

Applying these frameworks to AI poses a unique set of challenges. For instance, a utilitarian AI system might prioritize efficiency and overall well-being but could inadvertently marginalize minorities or individuals with unique needs. On the other hand, a deontological AI system might adhere strictly to rules but lack the flexibility to adapt to unforeseen or nuanced scenarios.

One approach to reconcile these viewpoints is to develop AI ethics committees or oversight bodies, comprised of experts from various fields—technology, ethics, law, sociology, and more. Such multi-disciplinary teams could provide a more balanced view and set guidelines that integrate different ethical principles.

The ethical considerations surrounding AI inevitably lead us to questions of regulation and governance. While self-regulation within the tech industry has its merits, it's increasingly clear that external oversight is necessary. However, there are challenges in legislating rapidly evolving technologies. By the time laws catch up, the technology may have already moved on, creating a regulatory lag.

Some countries and international bodies have started drafting AI-specific laws or have adapted existing legal frameworks to include AI. For instance, data protection laws like the GDPR[2] in the European Union incorporate some guidelines on automated decision-making. Still, there is much work to be done. The multi-faceted nature of AI ethics demands a collaborative global approach to regulation, one that takes into account cultural differences, economic inequalities, and geopolitical tensions.

2. https://gdpr-info.eu/

Ethical AI in Practice

Ethical considerations are not just theoretical but have real-world implications. Companies like IBM and Google have published their own AI ethics guidelines, emphasizing principles like fairness, accountability, and transparency. OpenAI, the organization behind this text generation model you're currently interacting with, has a Charter that focuses on ensuring that access to, benefits from, and influence over AI are widespread.

However, the gap between these lofty principles and everyday practice can be wide. High-profile cases have highlighted failures in AI ethics, such as biased facial recognition software or controversial military applications. These incidents serve as cautionary tales, emphasizing the importance of ethical oversight not just in the design phase but throughout an AI system's lifecycle.

Transparency in AI: The Black Box Problem

Transparency is another crucial ethical aspect of AI. One of the significant challenges in AI, particularly with complex models like neural networks, is their "black box" nature. While these models are highly effective in tasks like image recognition or natural language processing, it's often unclear how they arrive at a particular decision or conclusion.

This lack of transparency can have severe implications. In healthcare, for example, clinicians may be hesitant to act on an AI system's recommendations without understanding its reasoning. This can create a disconnect between technology and practice, negating some benefits that AI could bring.

Several methods are being developed to make AI systems more explainable, such as "LIME" (Local Interpretable Model-agnostic Explanations) and "SHAF" (Shapley Additive Explanations). These techniques aim to approximate complex models with simpler ones for individual predictions, providing insights into the model's decision-making process. However, there's a trade-off between accuracy and interpretability: more transparent models often perform less well than their "black box" counterparts.

Human oversight, commonly referred to as having a "Human-in-the-Loop," can serve as a check against machine-made decisions. This approach allows a human expert to review, modify, or override AI decisions, particularly in critical sectors like healthcare, criminal justice, and finance.

Having a Human-in-the-Loop could alleviate some ethical concerns, but it also poses new questions. For example, how much decision-making should be left to machines? If a human expert disagrees with an AI's recommendation, whose judgment should prevail? These are questions that we must grapple with as AI systems increasingly integrate into various industries.

Algorithmic Auditing: Holding AI Accountable

As AI systems proliferate, the call for accountability grows stronger. Algorithmic auditing is an emerging field that aims to scrutinize machine learning models. The objective is to identify any instances of unfairness, bias, or other ethical shortcomings and to understand the reasons behind such behavior. While it's a growing practice, the field is still in its infancy, and standard procedures and certifications are yet to be established.

Audits could become a requirement for AI systems, especially in sectors where the stakes are high, such as criminal justice or healthcare. However, auditing algorithms can be complicated and may require specialized skills that are currently scarce.

Impact on Developing Countries

The ethical implications of AI are not uniform globally; they have different ramifications depending on the socio-economic context. For example, countries with less access to technology may suffer from "algorithmic colonialism," where AI systems developed in wealthier nations are deployed in poorer ones without adaptation to local needs or conditions. This could exacerbate existing inequalities and create new forms of exploitation or discrimination.

By acknowledging the global disparities in AI's impact, we can start to formulate ethical guidelines that consider global justice and equality, rather than perpetuating the values of a particular region or group.

AI and Public Policy

Public policy has a significant role to play in shaping the ethical landscape of AI. Currently, there's a regulatory gap when it comes to AI technologies. Unlike traditional industries that have decades of laws and guidelines, the fast-paced evolution of AI technologies often leaves lawmakers struggling to keep up.

Because of this lag in legislation, some companies and researchers operate in a sort of "wild west," where the lack of stringent rules can lead to the implementation of AI systems with insufficient ethical oversight. This has led to calls for more comprehensive AI ethics policies, ranging from data protection laws to guidelines on AI in warfare.

The challenge in policymaking lies in balancing innovation with ethical considerations. Too stringent regulations may stifle technological advancements, while too lax oversight may lead to ethical transgressions that harm individuals and communities.

AI Ethics Committees

Several organizations and academic institutions are establishing AI ethics committees to provide guidance on the ethical development and deployment of AI technologies. These committees consist of multidisciplinary teams including computer scientists, ethicists, sociologists, and industry experts.

Their aim is to create a set of best practices for ethical AI development, sometimes even offering certification for AI systems that meet specified ethical criteria. However, the authority and effectiveness of these committees vary widely, and there is an ongoing debate about how to standardize ethical considerations across different sectors and geographical locations.

Social Considerations and Psychological Impacts

The interaction between AI systems and society extends far beyond mere transactional or functional aspects. There are significant psychological impacts to consider. For example, the way an AI system is designed can significantly affect human behavior. Social media algorithms that prioritize engagement can inadvertently contribute to the spread of misinformation or encourage polarization, affecting public discourse in profound ways.

Understanding these psychological impacts is vital for ethical AI design. It invites us to reconsider the metrics of success for AI systems, urging a move away from purely performance-based metrics like accuracy or speed to include the societal and psychological consequences of these technologies.

With AI technologies becoming an integral part of our daily lives, there is a growing need for AI literacy among the public. Understanding the basic workings and limitations of AI can empower individuals to make more informed decisions, whether its scrutinizing news articles generated by AI or questioning an AI system's decision in healthcare or legal matters.

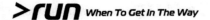

Education about AI ethics should start at an early age and be an integral part of the educational curriculum. Equipping future generations with the critical thinking skills to navigate an AI-driven world is not just beneficial—it's essential.

User Consent and Data Privacy

One of the most pressing concerns in AI ethics is user consent and data privacy. AI systems are notorious for their hunger for data, collecting everything from user behavior to personal information. This is particularly relevant in the context of IoT (Internet of Things) devices, smart homes, and wearables, which generate an enormous amount of data.

The issue of consent is multifaceted. Often, users may not fully understand the extent to which their data will be used, or how it will be processed by machine learning algorithms. Terms of service agreements are frequently long and complicated, making it easy for companies to bury important details in the fine print.

Given the sensitivity and potential misuse of personal data, there is a growing consensus around the need for clearer, more transparent consent mechanisms. Some argue for an "opt-in" rather than an "opt-out" system for data collection, requiring active consent from users before their data can be used.

The AI Accountability Gap

Accountability in AI is another area requiring urgent attention. When an AI system makes a decision, who is responsible? Is it the developer, the operator, the end-user, or the machine itself? This question becomes particularly challenging in the case of AI systems that "learn" from their interactions, evolving their behavior over time without human intervention.

The notion of accountability is intrinsically tied to the legal systems within which these technologies operate. However, current legal frameworks are often ill-equipped to deal with the complexities introduced by AI, leading to an "accountability gap."

Addressing this gap requires a multifaceted approach, including legislative efforts, the development of new accountability frameworks, and perhaps even the creation of a new field of "AI law." Nevertheless, it remains an ongoing challenge, with far-reaching implications for justice and social equality.

While much of the discussion around AI ethics is centered in developed countries, the ethical implications are even more profound in emerging economies. Issues of data privacy, consent, and accountability are magnified when considering less stringent regulatory environments or gaps in public understanding of technology.

Moreover, there's the potential for AI to exacerbate existing inequalities. For example, AI systems trained on data from developed countries may perform poorly when deployed in different cultural or socio-economic contexts, potentially leading to harmful or unfair outcomes.

It is crucial that the ethical discussion around AI includes diverse perspectives, taking into account different cultures, traditions, and levels of technological understanding. This inclusion ensures that AI serves as a tool for global betterment rather than an instrument of inequality.

Chapter 3: Navigating the Virtual Assistants

Virtual assistants like Siri, Alexa, and Google Assistant have become integral parts of our lives, helping us with everything from setting reminders to finding the nearest coffee shop. But as these AI-driven platforms become more sophisticated, a range of ethical and practical issues arise.

Siri, Alexa, and Google: A Comparative Analysis

Apple's Siri, Amazon's Alexa, and Google Assistant each have their own strengths and weaknesses. While Siri is deeply integrated into the Apple ecosystem, Alexa excels at smart home management, and Google Assistant is renowned for its search capabilities. However, the differences go beyond functionality. These platforms also differ in how they handle data, user privacy, and even in their approach to ethical considerations like bias.

The data handling policies of these companies are worth scrutinizing. Apple, for instance, emphasizes privacy and minimizes data collection. In contrast, Google collects a considerable amount of data to improve its services, which raises concerns about user privacy and potential misuse.

Voice recognition technology has come a long way, but it's not without its issues. For one, there is the risk of unauthorized voice commands. In a household where a smart speaker is used, anyone can potentially interact with the device, posing security risks.

Moreover, voice recognition algorithms aren't perfect and often struggle with accents or dialects. This has implications for fairness and inclusivity, as people from certain backgrounds might find these services less accessible or useful.

Perhaps one of the most unsettling questions surrounding virtual assistants is: Who's listening? These devices are designed to be always-on, ready to respond to your voice commands. However, this means they are constantly listening to ambient noise, which often includes private conversations. While companies assure users that no data is stored or sent without the activation phrase, instances of accidental activation have led to privacy violations.

Furthermore, there are concerns about the human reviewers employed by tech companies to improve voice recognition algorithms. These reviewers often listen to snippets of audio that could include sensitive or private information, posing ethical and privacy concerns.

As with many areas of AI, the fast-paced development of virtual assistants has outstripped the growth of corresponding legal frameworks. This puts the onus on companies to self-regulate, a situation that could be fraught with conflicts of interest.

Advocacy for stringent laws governing voice data collection and usage is gaining momentum. A key issue is how to balance the technological advancements that benefit society at large with the potential risks and ethical considerations. Recent regulatory proposals aim to bring more transparency and user control into this domain, but implementing such measures effectively remains a challenge.

The Ethical Conundrum: Virtual Assistants and Surveillance Capitalism

The relationship between users and virtual assistants isn't just one of service provider and consumer; it's increasingly becoming a focal point in the discussion about surveillance capitalism. This term, coined by Shoshana Zuboff, describes a new economic order where the commodity for sale is your personal data. Virtual assistants, always listening, represent a new frontier in the gathering of this invaluable resource.

Many don't realize the extent to which their data can be monetized. Your preferences, your location, your shopping habits—all of this can be extracted from your interactions with a virtual assistant and used to create a profile for targeted advertising or even predictive policing. This intensifies ethical concerns about data collection and misuse, adding a commercial angle to the privacy issues mentioned earlier.

Another intriguing angle is the emotional labor performed by these virtual assistants. Designed to engage us with human-like interaction, virtual assistants like Siri and Alexa often employ a female voice and are programmed to express politeness, understanding, and even hints of humor. However, these AI entities are not capable of feeling emotions. This creates a paradox where they are engaged in what traditionally has been considered emotional labor without the corresponding emotional experience.

The outsourcing of emotional labor to AI may have societal implications. For instance, as virtual assistants take on tasks like sending thank-you notes or apologizing, these "social lubricants" that smooth human interactions become automated, and potentially, less meaningful.

The absence of real emotional intelligence in virtual assistants presents its own set of challenges. While these platforms can perform tasks and provide information, they lack the nuanced understanding of human emotion that comes from lived experience. This has significant implications for their application in sensitive contexts like healthcare, where a failure to recognize emotional nuance could lead to misunderstandings and incorrect treatment recommendations.

Real emotional intelligence involves empathy, compassion, and the ability to recognize and respond to subtle emotional cues. The absence of these qualities in virtual assistants limits their functionality in settings that require emotional nuance and understanding.

The Influence on Children and Future Generations

As virtual assistants become a household norm, it's vital to consider the implications on younger generations. Children growing up with Alexa or Siri as a 'member' of the household are exposed to AI from a young age. What behaviors and attitudes might this instill? Will children learn to say 'please' and 'thank you' to AI, or will they become accustomed to barking orders at non-human entities without the need for politeness?

These questions don't have easy answers but are crucial to consider as virtual assistants become more integrated into our daily lives. Researchers and ethicists are already probing into the potential long-term effects of this interaction between AI and children.

The Gendered Nature of Virtual Assistants

The gendering of virtual assistants is a topic that often flies under the radar, but it's a significant issue in the realm of AI ethics. The majority of popular virtual assistants come with a default female voice and are often programmed with names that are traditionally feminine, such as Alexa and Siri. This raises concerns about the perpetuation of gender stereotypes, specifically the association of women with subservient roles and emotional labor.

The gender issue also intersects with cultural contexts. In some cultures, the use of a female voice for subservient tasks could reinforce regressive gender roles. Companies are gradually becoming aware of these concerns. Some are starting to offer a range of gender-neutral and male voices, but the conversation around this issue is still in its infancy.

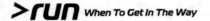

Regulation and Oversight

As AI systems continue to intertwine with our lives, the need for regulation becomes more pressing. Virtual assistants, being pervasive and personal, could serve as a litmus test for broader AI regulation. Several countries and international bodies are in the initial stages of crafting guidelines and laws aimed at governing the ethical considerations surrounding AI. For example, the European Union has proposed regulations that aim to create a 'trustworthy AI' by focusing on transparency and accountability.

Regulation is a double-edged sword. While it's necessary to ensure ethical compliance, excessive or poorly designed regulation could stifle innovation and make it harder for smaller companies to compete. Striking a balance is key.

The Dual Role of the User: Consumer and Product

It's important to realize that in the world of virtual assistants, the user plays a dual role. On one hand, you are the consumer, availing the services provided by these platforms. On the other, you are also the product, as your data is harvested, analyzed, and potentially sold or used for targeted advertising. This dual role complicates the ethics surrounding virtual assistants, as it's not just about the responsibility of the companies that create these technologies, but also about consumer awareness and education.

The Environmental Impact

A less-discussed but crucial aspect of the virtual assistant landscape is its environmental footprint. Data centers hosting these AI systems consume vast amounts of energy. While companies like Google and Amazon are investing in renewable energy sources, the overall energy consumption and carbon footprint of running sophisticated AI systems around the clock cannot be ignored. The convenience of asking a virtual assistant to turn on the lights may come at an environmental cost that society should be conscious of.

A Look into the Future: What Comes Next?

As machine learning algorithms grow more complex and computing power increases, virtual assistants will become more capable, perhaps even achieving a level of conversational ability indistinguishable from human beings. This will intensify all the ethical questions we've discussed so far, pushing society to urgently seek solutions.

The evolving nature of AI means that the ethical landscape is constantly shifting. Ongoing public discourse and academic research are essential for adapting our ethical frameworks to accommodate new challenges. Whether we'll master this balance effectively remains to be seen, but what is certain is that the interaction between ethics and AI will continue to be a defining narrative of our time.

As virtual assistants become an integral part of our daily lives, there is a pressing need for regulation and oversight to ensure that ethical considerations are addressed. Currently, tech companies operate in a relatively gray area when it comes to the governance of AI and data collection.

Governments and international organizations are beginning to catch up, but the pace is slow. For instance, the European Union has been more proactive with regulations like the General Data Protection Regulation (GDPR), setting a precedent for data privacy. Still, much needs to be done on a global scale, particularly in countries with less stringent laws on data protection.

Efforts to regulate should aim to strike a balance between innovation and ethical considerations. Over-regulation could stifle growth and development, but a lack of rules can lead to abuse and potentially harmful consequences. Collaborative dialogues between tech companies, policymakers, ethicists, and other stakeholders are crucial to formulating effective governance.

The Long-term Implications

Thinking long-term, we must consider the implications of a future where virtual assistants are ubiquitous, further advanced, and perhaps even integrated into our physical selves through bio-implants or other means. What does a society look like where AI not just assists but predicts and influences our every move? Will we become too reliant on these entities, consequently dulling our problem-solving skills and individual autonomy?

Moreover, the more we integrate these AI systems into our lives, the more data they accumulate. Years or decades down the line, these platforms will hold a lifetime's worth of personal information. The implications for data security and personal freedom are profound.

At the end of the day, while it's easy to point fingers at corporations or the technology itself, we as consumers also have a role to play. Vigilance in how we interact with these platforms, the permissions we grant, and the data we share is crucial. Additionally, critical thinking and public discourse about the ethical considerations of virtual assistants can contribute to better, more responsible technology.

Being responsible users also means holding tech companies accountable. Public pressure can lead to change. For instance, after concerns were raised about the 'always listening' aspect of some virtual assistants, companies were prompted to provide clearer privacy settings and options for manual activation of the device.

Conclusion

The ethical landscape of virtual assistants is neither black nor white; it's a complex interplay of various factors that need continuous examination and discussion. The benefits these systems offer are undeniable, but the ethical quandaries they pose are significant and multifaceted. Both companies and consumers have a responsibility to engage in ethical practices to ensure that the technology serves us, and not the other way around.

This chapter has aimed to provide a comprehensive overview of these issues, from the data privacy concerns to the psychological impact and the need for regulation and human responsibility. As virtual assistants continue to evolve, so too should our ethical frameworks.

Chapter 4: AI in Healthcare

From Diagnosis to Treatment

The medical landscape is undergoing a massive transformation thanks to artificial intelligence. No longer confined to academic journals or speculative fiction, AI's impact on healthcare is a reality. We're talking about algorithms that can analyze medical images with precision rivaling that of experienced radiologists. There are AI systems that sift through huge databases of clinical studies and patient records to recommend personalized treatment plans. These are not far-off, hypothetical scenarios; they're happening now.

However, as with any technological advancement, there are hurdles to overcome. One of the biggest challenges is data security and privacy. Health data is sensitive and often subject to strict regulations. When an AI system processes this information, questions about data ownership and the potential for misuse come to the forefront.

Human interaction and compassion are cornerstones of medical care. Nurses, doctors, and other healthcare professionals bring a level of emotional support that, currently, AI can't replicate. Can an algorithm console a patient after a severe diagnosis? Probably not. Therefore, it's essential to find a balance between technological efficiency and the irreplaceable human touch.

Ethical Concerns and Data Privacy

The medical field has stringent ethical guidelines, ranging from patient confidentiality to the moral considerations surrounding end-of-life care. AI applications that venture into these territories need to be designed with the utmost caution. For example, could an AI system be programmed to understand and adhere to the Hippocratic Oath, the ethical code that dictates "do no harm"?

The sharing and use of medical data raise additional ethical concerns. When an AI system predicts a patient's future medical conditions based on their health data, who owns that prediction? Should that information be shared with insurance companies, and if so, what are the ramifications?

Just like other areas where AI is making strides, the healthcare sector is also in dire need of comprehensive regulations. Organizations like the Food and Drug Administration (FDA) are beginning to provide guidelines for AI-powered medical technologies. Still, the policies are not yet robust enough to cover the wide-ranging applications and ethical dilemmas we face.

Continued oversight and ethical review boards comprising medical professionals, ethicists, and data scientists could be one way to approach this. The idea is to create a multi-disciplinary group that can address the ethical dimensions from various viewpoints.

Future of AI in Healthcare

The trajectory of AI in healthcare is promising. With ongoing advances in machine learning techniques and computational power, AI systems are poised to become an integral part of healthcare delivery. But the stakes are high. We're dealing with human lives, making it imperative that AI applications in healthcare are developed and deployed responsibly.

Considering the weighty implications, it's clear that AI in healthcare isn't just a technological issue but a deeply ethical one as well. Both the medical community and AI practitioners have a joint responsibility to ensure that as AI systems become more intelligent, they also become more ethical.

Artificial Intelligence is revolutionizing many sectors, but perhaps none as critically important as healthcare. Whether it's diagnostic imaging, personalized treatment plans, or predictive analytics, AI's capabilities in healthcare are multi-dimensional and far-reaching. This isn't just about technology getting better; it's about fundamental improvements in the quality of care, effectiveness of treatments, and even the management of chronic diseases.

The integration of AI in healthcare isn't a straightforward affair. It's a matter interwoven with complexities of data security, ethical guidelines, and the inevitable question of empathy in medical practice. As AI systems take on more roles in diagnosing conditions and suggesting treatments, the healthcare community, policymakers, and society at large have to consider new dimensions in ethical practices, data privacy, and the regulatory landscape.

So, let's dig deeper into the data security and privacy concerns. Healthcare data is perhaps the most personal and sensitive data about an individual. The management of this data by AI systems needs to be not just technically sound but ethically impeccable. When we talk about AI accessing vast health records to provide diagnostic recommendations, questions about data ownership, encryption, and patient consent become unavoidable. These questions aren't new, but they acquire a different complexity when AI is part of the equation.

And then there's the question of empathy. Can a machine ever replicate the emotional support that a healthcare professional provides? While AI can aid clinicians in more accurate diagnosis and effective treatment plans, it lacks the ability to understand human emotions. As we increasingly integrate AI into healthcare, we should consider ways to maintain the irreplaceable value of human touch. For instance, AI systems could be designed as a supplement to human care, rather than a replacement, ensuring that emotional and psychological factors are not overlooked.

Beyond the interpersonal aspect, AI's role in healthcare faces numerous ethical challenges that need to be rigorously addressed. Could an AI system, for instance, make an ethically sound judgment about end-of-life care for a patient? While technology may eventually answer this, ethical considerations are bound to guide how we allow AI to make such decisions. It raises important considerations about incorporating ethical norms into machine learning models used in healthcare, leading to discussions about 'ethical AI.'

The regulatory landscape is another critical aspect that we need to consider. As AI continues to break new ground in healthcare, it becomes crucial to have comprehensive and dynamic regulatory frameworks. Existing bodies like the Food and Drug Administration are making strides in this direction, but the speed at which AI is advancing makes it imperative to continually update these regulations.

In summary, the impact of AI on healthcare is profound, offering new avenues for diagnosis, treatment, and patient care. However, with these advancements come new questions and responsibilities concerning ethics, data privacy, and the inherent lack of emotional intelligence in AI systems. As we move forward, the integration of AI into healthcare will require a delicate balance between technological innovation and ethical consideration.

Another key area that needs attention in the realm of AI and healthcare is the question of accessibility. As AI technologies become more sophisticated and specialized, there's a risk of widening the gap between well-funded hospitals in urban areas and less privileged healthcare facilities in rural or underfunded areas. How can we ensure that the benefits of AI reach everyone equally, especially those in marginalized communities or in regions without abundant resources?

The question of accessibility doesn't just extend to healthcare institutions but also to the patient. For instance, how easy is it for an average patient to understand and interact with these new AI-powered systems? Here we intersect with the field of human-computer interaction. It's crucial that as AI systems become more integral to healthcare, they are also designed to be user-friendly, easy to understand, and accessible to people from different socio-economic and educational backgrounds.

Let's consider a hypothetical but plausible scenario. An AI model designed to diagnose skin cancer has been trained primarily on data from Caucasian patients. If this model is then applied universally, it may yield inaccurate results for patients from other ethnic backgrounds. This highlights the importance of diversity in data sets, an aspect that is often overlooked. It's not just a question of social fairness but of medical accuracy and life-saving efficiency.

The role of AI in healthcare is not merely confined to patient diagnosis and treatment. It has a significant role to play in administrative tasks, helping healthcare providers to manage records, billing, and even insurance claims more effectively. AI can streamline these processes, reduce errors, and allow healthcare professionals to focus more on patient care than on administrative tasks.

Moreover, AI can contribute to medical research. Whether it's in the identification of potential drug candidates or the analysis of clinical trial data, AI technologies can process and analyze large sets of data in ways human researchers cannot. For example, machine learning models can predict how different drugs interact, thereby significantly speeding up the drug development process.

However, as AI continues to expand its footprint in the healthcare sector, it also raises legitimate concerns about job displacement. While AI can take over some of the diagnostic and administrative tasks, what does that mean for the medical staff currently handling those jobs? It's important to view AI as a tool that can augment human skills rather than replace them. Reskilling and retraining will become critical components of integrating AI into healthcare, ensuring that the human workforce can work alongside these advanced technologies effectively.

AI is fundamentally transforming healthcare in ways we couldn't have imagined a few years ago. But this transformation brings with it an array of ethical, social, and logistical questions that require urgent attention. From data privacy to accessibility, from ethical considerations to job displacement, AI's role in healthcare is a double-edged sword that needs to be wielded carefully. As we continue to push the boundaries of what AI can achieve, it becomes imperative to tread cautiously and responsibly, ensuring that we harness the benefits while mitigating the risks.

Beyond the immediate medical applications, AI technologies also have the potential to revolutionize health education and training. Virtual Reality (VR) and Augmented Reality (AR), coupled with AI, could create more immersive and realistic training scenarios for medical professionals. Imagine a medical student practicing a complicated surgical procedure on a virtual patient, guided in real-time by an AI system that provides instant feedback, mimics real-life complexities, and even introduces unexpected complications to better train the student for real-life situations.

However, such advancements are not without challenges. One of the major issues is data security. As healthcare systems rely more on AI technologies, they also become more susceptible to cyber-attacks. The data being used isn't just any data; it's highly sensitive and personal medical data. Unauthorized access to this information could result in severe consequences, ranging from identity theft to the compromise of patient care. Hospitals and medical facilities will need to invest in robust security measures to protect against this vulnerability, adding another layer of complexity and cost to the healthcare system.

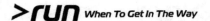

It's also crucial to address the 'digital divide' when implementing AI in healthcare. High-speed internet access and digital literacy are not universally available. While AI systems can make healthcare more efficient, we need to ensure that these benefits are accessible to people in remote or impoverished areas who might lack the necessary technological infrastructure. Efforts must be made to include these marginalized communities in the digitization of healthcare to prevent the further exacerbation of existing healthcare disparities.

In terms of regulation and oversight, the deployment of AI in healthcare presents a whole new set of challenges. How do we ensure that AI systems meet established medical standards and protocols? One possibility is the formation of a governing body, a consortium of AI experts, medical professionals, ethicists, and policymakers who can define guidelines and regulations for the development and deployment of AI in healthcare. This governing body could also be responsible for periodic audits and certifications, ensuring that AI technologies used in healthcare remain compliant with established standards and ethics.

Another dimension that we should consider is the long-term societal impact of AI in healthcare. While immediate benefits are evident, the long-term consequences are much harder to predict. For example, as AI systems become more advanced and ubiquitous, there could be a generational shift in the skill set required for future healthcare professionals. Understanding and interacting with AI could become as important as understanding human anatomy, possibly leading to an educational shift that focuses more on technological expertise than ever before.

Furthermore, the introduction of AI in healthcare is not solely a technological or scientific challenge but also an organizational one. The system needs to be integrated within existing healthcare structures, including administration, billing, and patient management. Health organizations may need to undergo a fundamental transformation, aligning their processes and workflows to better accommodate these new technologies. These adjustments aren't just costly but also time-consuming, posing a significant barrier to the adoption of AI.

AI's role in the mental health sector cannot be ignored. While the primary focus often remains on physical ailments and diseases, AI has the potential to make significant contributions to the treatment of mental health conditions. Chatbots designed to offer psychological support are already in use and could serve as a first line of assistance, especially in regions where professional help is scarce. These AI-powered solutions can engage with users, helping to manage stress, anxiety, and other mild mental health conditions, while escalating more severe cases to human professionals.

The question of data ownership is another complex issue. With AI systems churning through vast amounts of patient data to make accurate diagnoses and treatment plans, who owns this data? This is especially relevant when these A algorithms may discover new correlations or medical insights from the data they analyze. Do these discoveries belong to the developers of the AI, the healthcare institutions, or the patients themselves? Striking a fair balance in this domain will require thoughtful legal and ethical discussions.

Moreover, as AI systems learn and evolve, the concept of 'informed consent' for patients becomes increasingly complicated. Patients might consent to a particular treatment based on the current capabilities of an AI system. But what happens when that system upgrades and evolves? Can a patient be considered informed if the AI system itself is a moving target, continually updating its capabilities and methods?

Lastly, let's touch upon the human element in healthcare. While AI can perform a multitude of tasks, it lacks the ability to empathize. A machine cannot replicate the comforting touch of a nurse, the reassuring words of a doctor, or the empathetic ear of a psychologist. These human elements have immeasurable therapeutic value and contribute significantly to the healing process. Despite all its promise, AI should be seen as a tool that aids healthcare professionals, not as a replacement for the irreplaceable human touch.

Chapter 5: The Self-Driving Paradigm

The Evolution of Autonomous Vehicles

The journey from the first gasoline-powered car to today's self-driving vehicles is nothing short of remarkable. Over the past decade, autonomous vehicles (AVs) have moved from the realm of science fiction to our daily lives. Companies like Tesla, Waymo, and Cruise are in a race to perfect self-driving technology, each with its own approach to hardware and software. But it's not just technology companies that are invested; traditional automakers like Ford and GM are also heavily involved.

The push for autonomous driving comes from multiple fronts. On one hand, there's the appeal of increased safety. According to the National Highway Traffic Safety Administration (NHTSA), 94% of car accidents are caused by human error. Self-driving cars, theoretically, could significantly reduce such incidents. On the other hand, AVs promise to revolutionize our approach to mobility, especially for those unable to drive due to physical constraints.

The idea of a machine making life-or-death decisions is a topic that has ethical and legal complexities. One of the biggest questions around the deployment of autonomous vehicles is liability. In the case of an accident, who is responsible? Is it the driver, the car manufacturer, or the software developer? The legal landscape is still murky, with lawmakers struggling to keep up with the pace of technological advancement.

Moreover, there are ethical questions about how these vehicles should behave in emergency situations. The classic example is the "trolley problem," a hypothetical scenario where the vehicle has to choose between two bad outcomes. Would the car prioritize the safety of its passengers over pedestrians? Or should it follow a utilitarian approach, aiming to minimize overall harm?

These questions aren't just philosophical; they have real-world implications. In March 2018, a self-driving Uber car struck and killed a pedestrian in Arizona, sparking a nationwide debate on the ethics of autonomous vehicles. While the safety driver present in the car was found to be watching a video on her phone, the incident raised important questions about machine ethics and accountability.

Trust and the Human Element

One of the most significant hurdles for the widespread adoption of autonomous vehicles is trust. Many people are skeptical about handing over the control of a vehicle to a machine. There's an emotional aspect to driving that a machine can't replicate— the feel of the road, the experience of navigating through traffic, and the joy of a perfectly executed turn.

While manufacturers argue that autonomous vehicles will be safer, more efficient, and more convenient, convincing the public is another challenge altogether. Surveys have indicated a split opinion: while some people are excited about a future where they don't have to drive, others are deeply skeptical.

Even with advanced machine learning algorithms and extensive road testing, self-driving cars are not entirely foolproof. There have been instances where autonomous vehicles have made errors, sometimes with tragic outcomes. These incidents, though isolated, create a perception problem, making people question the technology's readiness and reliability.

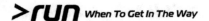

To foster trust, some companies are taking a gradual approach, introducing features like lane-keeping, adaptive cruise control, and parking assist before launching fully autonomous vehicles. The idea is to let people get accustomed to machine assistance in driving tasks, gradually building up to a point where the car can take over completely.

The Economic Impact

The implications of self-driving cars extend far beyond the realms of technology, safety, and ethics; they also have the potential to cause a seismic shift in our economy. Traditional jobs related to driving, such as trucking, taxi services, and delivery, could face disruption. According to a study by McKinsey, autonomous vehicles could eliminate up to 4.4 million driving jobs in the United States alone.

However, this doesn't mean that the advent of self-driving cars will result in mass unemployment. New roles will emerge in programming, maintenance, and data analysis. Companies specializing in AV technology will require specialized talent to design, build, and manage these vehicles. Additionally, self-driving cars could make transport more efficient, lowering costs for goods and services, thereby stimulating economic activity in other sectors.

Public Infrastructure and Policy

The rollout of self-driving cars won't occur in a vacuum. It will necessitate changes to existing infrastructure and the formulation of new public policies. Roads will need to be redesigned to accommodate autonomous vehicles, especially in densely populated urban areas where the integration of AVs poses a logistical challenge.

Government agencies will have to come up with policies and regulations that ensure the safe operation of self-driving cars. This will include specifying the required safety features, determining the guidelines for testing, and setting the standards for vehicle-to-vehicle communication. Cooperation between the public and private sectors will be essential in this regard.

Psychological and Cultural Shifts

Cars have always been more than just a means of transport; they've been an integral part of American culture. The idea of the "open road" is deeply embedded in the American psyche. How will this cultural attachment to driving change when machines take the wheel?

Autonomous vehicles will alter the psychology of mobility. The transition won't be straightforward. There will be a generation of drivers who find it difficult to let go of the control, and another that may never know how to drive a car manually. The cultural impact of this transition is difficult to predict but will undoubtedly be profound.

"The advent of autonomous vehicles raises numerous questions and considerations that society must grapple with. As we edge closer to a reality where machines manage mobility, a multidisciplinary approach involving automakers, tech companies, policymakers, and the public will be vital for ensuring a smooth and ethical transition."

Environmental Considerations

The potential environmental impact of self-driving cars is a complex issue with both positive and negative ramifications. On one hand, autonomous vehicles promise to optimize driving patterns, reducing fuel consumption and emissions. Their advanced algorithms can calculate the most efficient routes, adjust speed to minimize fuel usage, and reduce idling time.

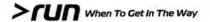
However, the rise of self-driving cars could also lead to a surge in the overall number of vehicles on the road. Easier and more convenient travel might encourage people to use cars more frequently, increasing the total miles driven and thus potentially offsetting any gains in fuel efficiency.

It's also worth considering the environmental cost of manufacturing these high-tech vehicles. The sensors, batteries, and advanced materials required for autonomous cars could put additional strain on our planet's resources. Thus, it becomes imperative for manufacturers to focus on sustainability, not just innovation, as they develop the next generation of autonomous vehicles.

Legal Landscape

The legal landscape surrounding self-driving cars is still a work in progress. While there have been some strides made in establishing regulatory frameworks, much remains to be done. Issues like liability in the case of an accident, data privacy, and even basic road rules for autonomous vehicles are yet to be fully fleshed out.

For instance, who is responsible if a self-driving car is involved in an accident? Is it the passenger, the owner, the manufacturer, or the developer of the car's software? Answering these questions will require a revamp of our existing legal systems and the creation of new laws that specifically address the complexities introduced by autonomous technology.

Another area warranting in-depth discussion is the data security and privacy implications of self-driving cars. These vehicles collect massive amounts of data to operate safely and efficiently—data that could be a goldmine for marketers but also a target for hackers. While most manufacturers employ state-of-the-art encryption methods to protect this information, no system is entirely foolproof.

The risk extends beyond the vehicle's software to the data storage and transmission infrastructures that support these advanced systems. A breach in any of these areas could not only compromise user data but also have serious safety consequences. Legislations and standards need to be implemented to guide the collection, storage, and utilization of data gathered by self-driving vehicles.

Public Perception and Trust

No technological advancement can be successful without public buy-in. Public perception of self-driving cars varies significantly. On one end are those excited by the prospect of a safer, more efficient future. On the other are skeptics concerned about relinquishing control to machines and the ethical quandaries that accompany this shift.

The autonomous vehicle industry must invest in public education and transparency to win societal trust. Live demonstrations, public test drives, and open forums can help dispel myths and answer pressing questions that the average person might have.

The Way Forward

The path to a future filled with autonomous vehicles is paved with both opportunities and challenges. It's a journey that necessitates the collaboration of various stakeholders—from technologists and ethicists to policymakers and the general public. As we move toward this exciting yet uncertain future, it is critical that we approach it with a measured, thoughtful, and ethical mindset.

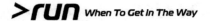

Environmental Impact

The potential for a positive environmental impact cannot be overlooked when discussing the transition to self-driving cars. Autonomous vehicles have the capability to optimize driving patterns, thereby reducing fuel consumption and emissions. If widely adopted, this could contribute significantly to the fight against climate change. However, this too comes with caveats. The manufacture and operation of highly sophisticated sensors and computers can offset these gains unless powered by renewable energy sources.

Infrastructure Overhaul

The successful integration of autonomous vehicles will also necessitate a comprehensive overhaul of existing infrastructure. Road signs, traffic lights, and even road surfaces may need to be adapted to facilitate machine vision and decision-making. Furthermore, communication systems need to be in place to allow for Vehicle-to-Vehicle (V2V) and Vehicle-to-Infrastructure (V2I) interactions, adding another layer of complexity to this evolutionary process.

Regulatory Landscape

As we navigate this unprecedented technological landscape, it is crucial that we have a robust regulatory framework to guide us. Legislation must keep pace with technological advancements to ensure that safety and ethical considerations are not compromised. Moreover, a standardized set of rules will enable manufacturers to design vehicles that are compliant, thereby expediting the adoption process.

Economic Implications

Lastly, we must consider the economic implications of a wide-scale transition to autonomous driving. While the technology has the potential to create new industries and job categories, it could also render several existing professions obsolete. Preparing the workforce for this transition through reskilling programs and other educational initiatives will be vital to ensuring that the benefits of autonomous driving are equitably distributed.

Concluding Remarks

While this chapter provides a comprehensive overview of the self-driving paradigm, it is by no means exhaustive. As with any technological revolution, the shift to autonomous driving presents a complex web of ethical, legal, and societal implications that warrant ongoing discussion. What remains constant is the need for a multi-faceted approach that brings together experts from diverse fields to navigate the road ahead responsibly and ethically. The journey to a self-driving future is fraught with both excitement and trepidation; how we navigate it will define our society for generations to come.

This concludes our exploration into the world of self-driving vehicles, but it is only a part of a broader conversation about the role of artificial intelligence in our lives.

Chapter 6: AI in the Workplace

Automation and Job Loss: A New Era or An Old Concern?

The conversation about the role of artificial intelligence (AI) in the workplace is as old as the technology itself. However, the anxiety around this topic has spiked significantly in recent years. As AI continues to mature, it's carving out its place in multiple sectors, and understandably, many are apprehensive about what this means for human jobs.

The dialogue around automation and job loss is often tinged with hyperbole. A multitude of reports and opinion pieces suggest that AI will replace a massive number of jobs, creating an employment crisis. The reality, as with most things, lies somewhere in the middle. While it's true that certain job functions, particularly those that are repetitive and don't require specialized skills, are at risk of automation, the whole picture is far more nuanced.

AI not only has the potential to replace certain tasks; it also creates new roles and reshapes existing ones. Consider the case of data analytics. A decade ago, the field didn't exist as it does today. With the advent of Big Data and advanced algorithms, a need emerged for skilled professionals who could interpret, analyze, and make actionable insights out of data. Thus, AI technology has created a new job market entirely.

Moreover, AI can serve as a complementary tool for many professions. Take the medical field, for example. AI systems can assist with diagnosing diseases or recommending treatments, but the doctor's expertise in understanding the patient's overall health context, emotional state, and other nuanced factors remains irreplaceable. In essence, AI can handle the data-crunching, leaving medical professionals to focus on more complex and humane aspects of healthcare.

42

Still, the threat to certain types of jobs is undeniable. Assembly line workers, data entry clerks, and even some levels of customer service could see significant impacts from automation. In these cases, upskilling becomes critical. Businesses, educational institutions, and governments need to collaborate on training programs that help workers transition into roles that machines can't easily assume.

The key question is not whether jobs will be lost, but how the job landscape will change and how we can prepare for it. Adaptation is a constant in human history; we have been adapting to technological changes for centuries. From the industrial revolution to the digital age, each technological leap has eradicated certain jobs but also created new opportunities. The advent of AI is no different; it is another chapter in the long story of human innovation and adaptability.

Augmenting Human Capabilities: The AI-Human Partnership

One of the most exciting aspects of AI in the workplace is its potential to augment human capabilities. While much attention is given to the jobs AI could replace, far less ink is spilled about how AI can make us more efficient, effective, and even creative in our roles.

Take the realm of decision-making, for example. Executives, managers, and team leaders often rely on a combination of data and intuition to make decisions. AI can play a pivotal role here by providing detailed, real-time analytics that illuminate patterns and trends that might not be otherwise apparent. Armed with this information, decision-makers can better evaluate their options and arrive at more informed conclusions.

In fields like design and architecture, AI can serve as a collaborative tool that helps professionals explore new forms, structures, and ideas. Algorithms can generate multiple design variations in a fraction of the time it would take a human, allowing the designer to select and refine the best ideas. Similarly, in the world of music and art, AI can assist in the creative process, serving as a sort of digital muse that provides inspiration and even contributes ideas for new compositions or artworks.

The use of AI to augment human capabilities isn't just confined to high-skilled jobs. In retail and service industries, AI can help employees provide better customer service by quickly retrieving customer histories, recommending personalized options, and even predicting future needs based on past behavior. In this sense, AI becomes a powerful tool for enhancing the customer experience, empowering employees to perform their roles with greater efficiency and personalization.

What's essential to understand is that augmenting human capabilities is not just about making tasks easier or more efficient. It's about expanding the scope of what's possible. It's about enabling humans to focus on tasks that require emotional intelligence, creative thinking, and deep expertise, while machines handle the more routine aspects of work. By working in tandem, humans and machines can achieve outcomes neither could accomplish alone.

The AI-Human Workforce: Collaboration or Conflict?

The future of the workplace is not an "us vs. them" scenario where humans and machines are pitted against each other. Rather, it's shaping up to be a collaborative environment where each brings unique strengths to the table. But, like any relationship, the AI-human partnership comes with its own set of challenges and considerations.

Firstly, there's the issue of trust. Many people are understandably skeptical about the reliability of AI systems, especially when these systems are used in high-stakes or sensitive areas like healthcare, law enforcement, or financial services. This skepticism isn't unfounded; despite their capabilities, AI systems are not infallible. They can make mistakes, and when they do, the consequences can be severe.

To mitigate these concerns, organizations need to build robust governance frameworks around the use of AI. These frameworks should outline clear guidelines for human intervention and oversight. For instance, in a healthcare setting, any diagnosis made by an AI system should be reviewed and confirmed by a medical professional before any action is taken.

There's also the challenge of data privacy and security. As AI systems require vast amounts of data to function effectively, organizations must be vigilant in protecting this data to ensure it doesn't fall into the wrong hands or be used unethically. This responsibility doesn't lie with the IT department alone; it's a company-wide concern that requires continuous effort and vigilance from all employees.

Finally, there's the question of job redesign. As AI systems take on more tasks, the nature of certain jobs will change. Some roles may become obsolete, but new ones will also be created. The challenge for organizations is to manage this transition smoothly, ensuring that employees are adequately trained and prepared for the changes ahead.

To sum up, the impact of AI on the workplace is multifaceted. On one hand, it poses genuine risks and challenges that need to be thoughtfully addressed. On the other, it offers unprecedented opportunities for enhancing productivity, fostering innovation, and opening up new avenues for human creativity and collaboration.

It's not a question of if AI will change the workplace, but how. The answer lies in how well we understand this transformative technology and how judiciously we integrate it into our professional lives. Through proactive planning, ethical considerations, and a focus on augmenting human capabilities rather than replacing them, we can navigate this new terrain successfully. After all, the goal isn't to pit machines against humans but to create a harmonious workspace where both can coexist and thrive.

Ethics and Fairness: The Dark Side of AI in the Workplace

Ethical considerations are at the forefront of any discussion regarding the deployment of AI in the workplace. Often, the focus is on data privacy, but there's another critical aspect that demands attention: fairness.

AI systems are only as good as the data they are trained on. If the data contains biases, the AI system will likely perpetuate those biases. For instance, an AI system designed to sort through job applications could inadvertently favor candidates from certain backgrounds if the training data reflects such a bias. Therefore, it's crucial to examine the ethical underpinnings of AI deployments closely.

Ethics isn't just a concern for those programming the AI but for everyone in the organization. Creating an ethical AI system requires a multi-disciplinary approach, involving not just technologists but ethicists, sociologists, and other experts who can provide a broader perspective on the implications of the technology. Organizations need to adopt ethical frameworks for AI that focus on ensuring fairness, transparency, and accountability.

AI's Impact on Mental Health and Well-Being

Another often overlooked aspect of AI in the workplace is its potential impact on mental health. The relentless pace at which AI systems can work might set unrealistic expectations for human employees. There's also the anxiety that comes with the idea that a machine could replace you at any moment. Such stressors can't be ignored and need to be managed proactively.

Mental well-being is a shared responsibility. Organizations need to provide the necessary resources and environments where employees can discuss their concerns openly. Mental health programs, stress management seminars, and other employee wellness initiatives can go a long way in alleviating AI-induced stress and anxiety.

46

The Legal Landscape: Navigating Uncharted Waters

The rapid development and adoption of AI also raise several legal questions that have yet to be thoroughly addressed. Who is responsible if an AI system makes a mistake that has legal repercussions? What kind of rights do employees have if they feel they have been unfairly treated by an AI system?

Understanding and navigating the legal landscape around AI is crucial for any organization that plans to integrate this technology into its operations. Legal experts should be involved from the early stages of planning and implementation, and organizations must keep abreast of any changes in legislation that could impact their use of AI.

The future of AI in the workplace is not an isolated journey; it's a collaborative effort that involves multiple stakeholders, including employees, management, the technology community, legal experts, and even society at large. The goal should be to create a balanced ecosystem where AI can augment human capabilities and contribute positively to organizations without causing undue harm or ethical concerns.

Understanding the complexities and nuances of this topic is vital for any organization venturing into AI. As we've explored, the issues are numerous, ranging from automation and job loss to ethics and legal concerns. But so are the opportunities. With thoughtful planning, ethical considerations, and a collaborative spirit, the AI-human partnership can pave the way for an unprecedented era of innovation and workplace harmony.

Automation and Job Loss

While the fear of job loss due to automation is real and widely discussed, we must also consider the types of jobs we're talking about. It's crucial to differentiate between the loss of low-skilled jobs and high-skilled jobs. AI technology tends to target repetitive, manual labor initially. These are jobs that many argue humans shouldn't be doing in the first place, as they can be dangerous, degrading, or both. For example, manufacturing jobs have been on a steady decline in Western countries for decades due to automation. Machines don't need breaks, they don't form unions, and they don't get tired. They can perform repetitive tasks much more efficiently than humans, often with fewer errors. In many respects, this is a good thing. Dangerous jobs, like handling hazardous materials or working in extreme conditions, can be automated to protect human workers.

However, what happens to the displaced workers? Some argue that automation creates new jobs while eliminating old ones. While this might be true to an extent, there's a catch. The new jobs often require skills that the displaced workers don't possess, leading to the "skills gap." Upskilling is the obvious solution, but it's not as simple as it sounds. Training programs can be expensive and time-consuming, and there's no guarantee of a job at the end. For older workers, the prospect of going back to school to learn new skills can be daunting, if not impossible. Additionally, it's crucial to consider the psychological impact of job loss. A job is not just a means to earn money; it often provides a sense of identity and purpose. The loss of a job, therefore, can lead to a loss of self-worth, which is a serious issue that goes beyond economics.

Augmenting Human Capabilities

Amidst the concerns about job loss, it's essential to remember that AI can also work alongside humans to augment their capabilities. Take the medical field, for instance. AI-driven diagnostic tools can analyze medical images with incredible accuracy, but they don't replace doctors. Instead, they serve as invaluable aids that help medical professionals make more accurate diagnoses. The same goes for customer service. Chatbots can handle routine queries, freeing up human agents to deal with more complex issues that require emotional intelligence and nuanced understanding. This is a win-win situation where both the machine and the human agent are playing to their strengths.

Let's also not forget that AI can make jobs more enjoyable. Tasks that are repetitive and mundane can be automated, allowing human workers to focus on more creative and intellectually stimulating aspects of their work. For example, data entry is a tedious but necessary task in many industries. Automating this process can free up employees to engage in more strategic activities, such as data analysis and decision-making, which are not only more interesting but also add more value to the company.

AI also has the potential to make the workplace more inclusive. Voice recognition and natural language processing technologies can make software and applications more accessible to people with disabilities, removing barriers to employment for a significant portion of the population. The visually impaired, for instance, can benefit from AI-driven tools that can describe the world around them, while those with mobility issues can control computers and machinery through voice commands or even brain-machine interfaces.

The future of work is not necessarily humans versus machines, but rather, humans with machines. The symbiosis of human and machine can lead to unprecedented levels of productivity and innovation. As AI systems become more sophisticated, they could even learn to understand individual human preferences and working styles, creating a more personalized and efficient work environment. Companies that can successfully integrate AI into their workforce stand to gain a significant competitive advantage.

The discussion on AI's role in the workplace is far-reaching and needs further exploration. Issues like the governance of AI at work, the ethical considerations of employee surveillance, and the changing dynamics of team collaborations in an AI-augmented environment all merit detailed discussions.

Let's continue to delve deeper into these critical areas to offer a comprehensive view of AI's complex relationship with the workplace, both today and in the future.

Governance and Policy in the AI-Augmented Workplace

The implementation of AI technologies in the workplace inevitably raises questions about governance and policy. Who decides what tasks should be automated? What is the protocol for data privacy and ethical considerations when AI is monitoring the workforce? In many organizations, the rush to adopt AI technologies has preceded the establishment of clear governance models, creating gray areas that can be problematic.

For instance, data governance is a significant concern. AI systems require vast amounts of data to operate effectively. In the context of the workplace, this data often includes sensitive employee information. How is this data stored, who has access to it, and how is it used? Without clear policies, organizations run the risk of breaching privacy norms, either intentionally or unintentionally.

Data governance also extends to the AI algorithms themselves. Algorithms can be biased, reflecting the limitations or prejudices of their human creators. In a workplace setting, this can have serious implications. An AI system used for hiring, for example, could inadvertently discriminate against certain groups of people if it's not properly designed and managed. Therefore, organizations must establish clear policies around algorithmic fairness, transparency, and accountability.

Employee Surveillance and Ethical Considerations

Another pressing issue is the ethical implications of using AI for employee surveillance. With capabilities such as facial recognition, location tracking, and even sentiment analysis, AI technologies can provide employers with unprecedented levels of oversight. While this might have advantages in terms of productivity and security, it raises ethical questions about employee privacy and autonomy. Where do we draw the line between reasonable oversight and invasive surveillance?

Moreover, constant surveillance can have a detrimental impact on employee morale. Trust is a two-way street. If employees feel like they're always under scrutiny, they may become disengaged, anxious, or even resistant to AI technologies that are meant to help them. Thus, a delicate balance must be struck to ensure that AI serves as a tool for empowerment rather than oppression.

Changing Dynamics of Team Collaborations

As AI systems become more integrated into the workforce, they will inevitably change the way teams collaborate and work together. AI could take over specific roles within a team, such as data analysis or scheduling, freeing up human team members to focus on strategic planning and creative tasks. While this may improve efficiency, it also changes the interpersonal dynamics of the workplace. Team members will need to adapt their communication and problem-solving skills to work effectively in this new hybrid environment. This adjustment period could be challenging for some, especially those who are less tech-savvy.

Moreover, as AI technologies become smarter, there may be a temptation to let the machine make more of the decisions, gradually eroding human agency. Ensuring that team members remain engaged and empowered in an AI-augmented workplace is critical. Training programs must be put in place to help employees adapt to this new working environment, and organizational cultures must evolve to place a premium on human skills like creativity, emotional intelligence, and critical thinking.

AI and the Gig Economy

The growing gig economy, characterized by freelance, temporary, and short-term contracts, is another area where AI is having a significant impact. AI algorithms are already used to match freelancers with suitable jobs on platforms like Upwork and Fiverr. These algorithms analyze a myriad of factors, such as skills, experience, and even the language in which a freelancer communicates to determine the best fit for a particular job. While this can make the job-matching process more efficient, it raises questions about fairness and the potential for algorithmic bias.

Additionally, AI could potentially disrupt the gig economy by automating many of the tasks that freelancers currently perform. As AI technologies become more advanced, the range of jobs that can be automated will likely expand, possibly reducing opportunities for human workers in the gig economy.

The Road Ahead

The future of AI in the workplace is both exciting and fraught with challenges. While there is undoubtedly immense potential for positive change, there are also significant risks and ethical considerations that must be carefully managed. The key to a successful future lies in proactive governance, ethical considerations, and a focus on augmenting rather than replacing the human workforce. As organizations and employees navigate this evolving landscape, continuous learning, adaptation, and a commitment to ethical principles will be crucial.

While automation and job loss are significant concerns, one should not overlook the role AI plays in reskilling employees. Companies have started using AI-driven platforms for personalized learning experiences. These platforms use machine learning algorithms to assess the skill set of each employee and create a custom learning path to bridge the skill gap. In this way, AI doesn't just eliminate jobs; it also helps employees adapt to new roles that are often more aligned with their aptitudes and interests.

Mental Health and Productivity

AI's role in the workplace is not just confined to task automation and reskilling. Increasingly, companies are using AI-driven tools to assess and improve the mental health of their employees. Given the overwhelming stress levels in modern corporate culture, AI systems can monitor work patterns, behavior, and communication styles to identify stress points and recommend possible solutions. For instance, an AI program could analyze an employee's calendar and suggest more efficient scheduling to avoid back-to-back meetings and provide breathing space.

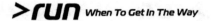

The Future of Remote Work and AI

The pandemic has accelerated the trend of remote work, and AI has been pivotal in facilitating this transition. AI-powered video conferencing tools, workflow automation systems, and even 'smart' home offices have made it easier for employees to maintain productivity while working from home. Additionally, AI analytics can help managers monitor performance and deliver real-time feedback, all while respecting the privacy and autonomy of remote workers.

AI and Organizational Behavior

AI's most profound impact may lie in how it changes the structure and behavior of organizations. Flat organizational structures are becoming more common, with AI taking over the role of middle management in some cases. The use of AI in decision-making processes can lead to a more democratic work environment where employees at all levels have a say. Moreover, AI algorithms can assess and predict the effectiveness of teams, facilitating better team compositions and, consequently, better outcomes.

The AI-Human Workforce: A Partnership, Not a Rivalry

A commonly perpetuated myth is that AI and humans are rivals in the workplace. But the most progressive organizations view them as partners. An AI algorithm can sort through thousands of emails to flag the most important ones, but it lacks the human touch needed to build relationships with clients or stakeholders. Similarly, a machine might diagnose an issue in a manufacturing unit, but it requires human expertise to solve it creatively. Therefore, the future of work is not humans vs. machines, but humans with machines.

The Integration Challenge

Despite the potential benefits, integrating AI into the workplace is not without challenges. Apart from the substantial financial investment, companies also need to consider the ethical implications. Data privacy is a major concern, especially when AI algorithms are monitoring employee behavior and performance.

To successfully integrate AI into the workplace, organizations need comprehensive guidelines and policies that employees understand and agree with. Transparency is essential to gain the trust of the workforce.

AI as an Inclusive Technology

In recent years, organizations have turned to AI as a means to foster inclusivity and diversity. AI can help reduce unconscious biases in recruitment by analyzing multiple data points to select the most suitable candidates, irrespective of gender, ethnicity, or other subjective factors. AI tools can also help make workplaces more accessible for people with disabilities. For example, AI-powered speech recognition software can transcribe meetings in real-time, assisting those with hearing impairments.

The AI Readiness Gap

Not all companies are on the same page when it comes to AI adoption. There's a palpable gap between companies that have the resources and know-how to implement AI effectively and those that don't. This AI readiness gap can be detrimental, as late adopters will find it increasingly difficult to catch up with their AI-savvy competitors. Businesses, especially small and medium-sized enterprises (SMEs), must therefore assess their capabilities and take proactive steps to bridge this gap.

Scalability and Customization

One of the biggest advantages of AI is its scalability. Organizations can start small, with one or two automated processes, and gradually scale their AI efforts as they become more comfortable and understand the technology better. Customization is also a significant advantage, as AI algorithms can be tailored to fit the unique requirements of each business, enhancing their operational efficiency.

Algorithmic Decision-making: Boon or Bane?

While AI can make faster and more accurate decisions based on data analytics, there's an ongoing debate about the level of autonomy that should be given to algorithmic decision-making systems. A balance must be struck between AI decision-making and human oversight to avoid the pitfalls of over-automation and to maintain the human touch in business operations.

Final Remarks

As we delve deeper into the AI era, businesses need to adapt to keep up with the pace of innovation. They face not only technical challenges but also ethical and organizational ones. Despite the hurdles, the potential benefits of implementing AI in the workplace are too significant to ignore. Organizations that manage to navigate these complex waters successfully will undoubtedly have a competitive edge in the market.

Chapter 7: The Social Impact of AI

Discrimination and Social Bias

In a world where AI algorithms touch upon almost every aspect of our lives, the issue of discrimination and social bias cannot be overstated. These algorithms, designed by humans and trained on historical data, can perpetuate existing prejudices, creating a vicious cycle that marginalizes certain communities. Whether it's racial bias in facial recognition software or gender bias in hiring algorithms, these technologies can pose real-world consequences.

Let's take the example of AI in the criminal justice system. There are algorithms designed to predict the likelihood of a defendant reoffending. While this might seem like a technological advancement aimed at assisting judges, these algorithms can be inherently biased. They may consider factors like zip codes, which are often correlated with racial and economic lines, thus perpetuating systemic inequalities. The fairness of an AI system in this context is not just a theoretical question; it has significant repercussions for social justice.

The AI Divide: Accessibility and Inclusion

Accessibility and inclusion are another crucial frontier in AI's social impact. As AI technologies become more advanced and integrated into our daily lives, there's a growing concern that these benefits will not be distributed equally. People who cannot afford smartphones or don't have access to high-speed internet are at risk of being left behind. In developing countries, the digital divide can be even more pronounced. Simple tasks like online banking, which have moved towards more complex authentication techniques involving AI, can become a hurdle for people without access to the required technology.

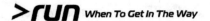

In education, we already see the beginnings of an AI divide. Wealthy school districts can afford sophisticated AI-driven analytics and personalized learning platforms, while underfunded schools struggle with basic facilities. This discrepancy raises ethical questions about the role of technology in widening social and economic gaps.

The Future of Social Interactions

As AI becomes more integrated into social platforms and online communities, we need to consider its impact on human interaction. Virtual assistants like Siri, Alexa, and Google Assistant are making the jump from mere task-performers to more interactive and "conversational" entities. These AI systems can engage users in natural language dialogue, making them more like a companion than a tool. The implications for loneliness, social skills, and interpersonal relationships are still under scrutiny. But as these platforms evolve, they may redefine the way we interact with technology and, by extension, each other.

It's not just about chatbots and virtual assistants. AI is starting to shape our social experiences in online communities and social media platforms. Algorithms determine what we see on our feeds, who we get connected with, and what content gets our attention. While these algorithms aim to keep us engaged, they can also create echo chambers, where we're only exposed to opinions similar to our own, leading to polarization.

Emotional AI and Empathy

The next frontier in AI's social impact is emotional AI or affective computing. These are systems capable of recognizing human emotions through facial expressions, voice modulation, and other physiological signals. Such capabilities can be harnessed for various applications—from customer service bots that can adapt their responses based on the emotional state of the user to mental health apps that can monitor emotional well-being.

However, the concept of machines understanding human emotion raises ethical and philosophical questions. Would such systems genuinely "understand" human emotion, or would they simply be very good at mimicking empathy? Could they manipulate our emotions for commercial or more nefarious purposes?

Social Robots and Companionship

Robotic pets and companions have been a subject of fascination and research for years, but advances in AI have brought us closer to making them a reality. Companies are already offering social robots that can carry on conversations, recognize family members, and even help with household chores. While the idea of robotic companions can be exciting, especially for lonely or elderly individuals, it also brings up a host of ethical and social questions. Would people start preferring the company of these programmed entities over real human interaction? Could these robots be used to replace human caregivers, and if so, what would we be losing in the process?

Community Surveillance and Social Scoring

In some countries, AI and surveillance technologies have been combined to create social scoring systems. Individuals are rated based on a variety of factors such as financial stability, social interactions, and even moral behavior. These scores can affect everything from loan eligibility to job opportunities. Such systems can have a chilling effect on individual freedoms and social dynamics. They can encourage conformity at the cost of individuality and critical thought.

Cultural Impact

AI's reach also extends into cultural domains. From algorithms that can write poetry and compose music to those that can paint and design, the cultural sector is ripe for disruption. But what does this mean for human artists? Are we delegating our cultural and creative responsibilities to algorithms, and if so, at what cost?

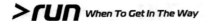

By impacting how we interact, work, and even think, AI is shaping our social fabric in ways we are only beginning to understand. While these technologies offer unprecedented opportunities for social development, they also pose significant ethical challenges that society must address.

Social Governance and Policy

The governance of AI technologies is a complex challenge that involves multiple stakeholders, including governments, the private sector, and civil society. There's an urgent need for a comprehensive framework that can guide the development and deployment of AI in a way that maximizes its benefits while minimizing its social costs.

As AI continues to permeate various sectors, it is crucial for policymakers, technologists, and the general public to engage in open dialogues about its social implications. Only through collective action can we ensure that AI serves as a force for good, enriching our lives while preserving the social values we hold dear.

The AI Divide: Accessibility and Inclusion

One of the most significant challenges society faces when integrating AI is the divide it creates between those with access to advanced technologies and those without. While many might think that this divide is solely a problem for the developing world, it's much more pervasive and exists in developed nations too. Even within prosperous countries, rural communities often suffer from a lack of access to advanced medical diagnostics or educational tools powered by AI.

The social divide can manifest in many forms: geographic, economic, or educational. While AI promises to automate many mundane tasks, enhance medical diagnostics, and improve educational outcomes, these benefits often flow to the most affluent sections of society first. What happens to those left behind? How do we ensure that the benefits of AI are distributed more evenly across various social strata?

Discrimination and Social Bias

Equally critical is the AI's potential for social bias and discrimination. As we touched upon in the ethics chapter, machine learning algorithms learn from existing data. When this data includes societal prejudices, whether they relate to race, gender, or economic status, the AI model is at risk of perpetuating or even exacerbating these prejudices. The extent of this issue is still not fully understood, but it's a problem that researchers and policymakers are starting to pay more attention to.

There are numerous examples where AI applications have shown discriminatory behavior. From sentencing algorithms that are biased against minority populations to facial recognition technologies that perform poorly on non-white, non-male faces, the risks are not trivial. Even in advertising algorithms, unintentional biases can lead to targeting job or housing ads based on race or gender. This has a ripple effect on the broader social structure, reinforcing existing inequalities and creating new forms of discrimination.

The Future of Social Interactions

AI is also shaping the future of human interactions in ways we might not yet fully appreciate. Virtual assistants and chatbots are increasingly sophisticated, capable of handling more complex tasks and conversations. While this has clear benefits, such as more efficient customer service or support for mental health, there is a trade-off in terms of human contact. As AI takes on more roles traditionally held by humans, there is the potential for a decrease in the kind of organic social interactions that are crucial for emotional and psychological well-being.

Even social media platforms, now powered by advanced machine learning algorithms, influence the way we interact. They are designed to keep users engaged, often showing them a narrow band of content that aligns with their existing beliefs and likes. This can result in a sort of digital tribalism where people are not exposed to diverse viewpoints or new information, hindering social development on a broader scale.

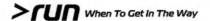

The AI's Impact on Democracy

Democracies thrive on open debate, shared facts, and the ability to agree to disagree. However, AI-driven algorithms can create information echo chambers, as stated earlier. This has more far-reaching consequences than just social interactions; it affects the democratic fabric of society.

AI can be employed to sway public opinion, manipulate voters, and even rig elections. Technologies like deepfakes can fabricate realistic videos, making it appear as though political figures are saying things they never did. This type of manipulation can have a profound impact on how people perceive information, further deepening social divides and undermining trust in democratic institutions.

While some countries are experimenting with AI in governance to make administrative procedures more efficient, the risks are considerable. A transparent, accountable human being can be replaced by a black box algorithm, making it harder to question or understand the decision-making process in governance. How these technologies are implemented in the public sector should be a matter of public debate, not just a technical one.

Collective Intelligence and Crowd Wisdom

On a more positive note, AI has the potential to elevate our collective intelligence. Systems that combine human and machine intelligence could offer new ways to tackle complex social issues like climate change, healthcare, and global inequality. Already, collaborative initiatives are using AI to analyze data and generate solutions that would be impossible or take much longer to achieve with human cognition alone.

Crowdsourcing wisdom through AI can offer new pathways for social innovation. Imagine a po icy decision supported not just by a handful of experts but by a nuanced machine learning model trained on diverse data, including social, economic, and environmental factors. Such a decision-making system would not replace human governance but augment it, offering data-driven insights that could be debated and refined by the public.

The Role of Education and Public Awareness

While policymakers, researchers, and corporations have a significant role in steering the social impact of AI, public awareness and education are equally crucial. A well-informed public is more likely to engage in meaningful debates and hold decision-makers accountable. Education should not be limited to explaining what AI can do but also delve into the ethical and social implications of these technologies.

Courses in schools and community centers, public debates, and even media coverage can contribute to a more nuanced understanding of AI's potential and pitfalls. We must move from a society that merely consumes AI services to one that questions, understands, and ultimately directs the technology's development in a socially responsible manner.

Economic Disruptions and Job Markets

Another social domain profoundly affected by AI is the job market. While automation and technology have always been drivers of economic change, the pace at which AI can potentially replace human tasks is staggering. Unlike previous industrial revolutions, the AI revolution is not merely substituting muscle with machinery; it's replacing complex cognitive tasks.

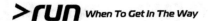

This poses a challenge to both low-skill and high-skill jobs. From manufacturing to data analysis, from driving to legal research, AI systems can either replace or significantly reduce the need for human intervention. How society adapts to this monumental shift could be a defining feature of the coming decades. Will we see massive unemployment, or will new kinds of jobs emerge? How prepared are we to retrain millions of people?

Some economists and futurists propose solutions like Universal Basic Income (UBI), where every citizen receives a set amount of money regardless of employment, effectively providing a safety net. The idea is to give people the freedom to retrain or engage in more creative, entrepreneurial activities without the fear of financial ruin. Yet, UBI is still a subject of heated debate with concerns about inflation, reduced incentives to work, and the sheer financial feasibility of such an endeavor.

Another proposed solution is the "job guarantee" programs, where the government assures a job for everyone who wants to work. While this could take many forms, from infrastructure projects to caregiving roles, it demands significant administrative oversight and could potentially create "make-work" jobs that don't contribute meaningfully to society.

What is clear is that transitioning to an AI-driven economy requires a multi-pronged approach, involving not just economic policies but also educational reforms, healthcare adjustments, and possibly even changes to how we define "work" in the first place.

Mental Health in the AI Age

The psychological impacts of AI are still an under-researched area, but early indications suggest a need for concern. As AI systems become more integrated into our daily lives, from social media algorithms to virtual assistants, they have the potential to affect our mental well-being. For example, the "always-on" culture perpetuated by constant connectivity can lead to increased stress and anxiety. AI algorithms that maximize user engagement on platforms contribute to the so-called "doom scrolling," where individuals keep consuming negative news, further exacerbating mental health issues.

Moreover, as AI takes on more roles—from customer service representatives to even therapists—there is the question of how these interactions impact our psychological health. Human contact, empathy, and the nuances of social interaction cannot be fully replicated by a machine. Relying on AI for emotional support or guidance may offer a convenient solution but could be psychologically detrimental in the long term.

Thus, it becomes essential to strike a balance and set boundaries for AI's role in mental health. While AI can assist in diagnostic procedures and even help in tracking mental health metrics, the human element—physicians, therapists, and counselors—should remain irreplaceable in the therapeutic process.

AI and the Arts: Creativity Reimagined

One of the most intriguing debates around AI's social impact is its role in the arts and creative endeavors. AI algorithms can now compose music, paint pictures, and even write stories. This blurs the line between human and machine creativity, posing existential questions about what makes us unique as a species.

While some argue that AI in the arts could democratize creativity, making it accessible for everyone to compose music or create art, others see a loss of the 'soul' or 'essence' that defines human-made art. There's also the question of ownership and copyright. Who owns the rights to a painting created by an AI? Is it the programmer, the operator of the machine, or the machine itself?

Artists themselves have mixed feelings. Some see AI as just another tool in their creative arsenal, much like a paintbrush or a musical instrument. Others worry that AI could trivialize the creative process, making it a commodity that can be mass-produced, with less value placed on human creativity.

However, it's worth noting that every significant technological advancement, from the printing press to the camera, has faced similar criticisms. Over time, society finds a balance, integrating the new technology into existing frameworks, but the transition can be turbulent.

Ethical Implications and Regulation

As we navigate the sea of challenges that AI presents, one of the most crucial aspects to consider is ethics. With AI's potential to outperform humans in a multitude of tasks, there arises the risk of its misuse. How do we ensure the ethical deployment of such a potent tool?

Firstly, there's the question of bias. AI systems, especially machine learning models, are only as unbiased as the data they are trained on. If historical data contain systemic prejudices, AI can perpetuate and even exacerbate these issues. For instance, facial recognition software has been found to be less accurate for people with darker skin tones, posing significant risks when employed in law enforcement.

Secondly, there's the issue of accountability. When AI systems make decisions, who is responsible for them? Is it the developers who coded the algorithm, the data scientists who trained the model, or the companies that deploy them? As we integrate AI into critical sectors like healthcare, transportation, and national security, the stakes get exponentially higher.

Thirdly, the question of privacy and surveillance looms large. AI's capabilities in data analytics, pattern recognition, and predictive modeling make it a powerful tool for monitoring and tracking. While this can have applications like fraud detection and national security, it can also lead to Orwellian scenarios of mass surveillance and loss of individual privacy.

To manage these ethical challenges, calls for AI regulation are getting louder. The European Union has been pioneering efforts in this regard, setting guidelines for trustworthy AI. However, the fluid and evolving nature of AI technology makes regulation a complex task. Too stringent laws could stifle innovation, while too lax an approach could risk ethical mishaps. Striking the right balance is crucial, but difficult.

International Relations and Geopolitical Impacts

The rise of AI has profound implications on international relations as well. As countries vie for dominance in this new technological frontier, we are seeing an increasingly polarized world where access to AI can be a determining factor in a nation's economic and military power. The AI race is not just a matter of national pride; it's a strategic imperative.

Global partnerships and collaborations in AI research are more critical than ever, but they are a so becoming increasingly complicated due to geopolitical tensions. While countries like the United States and China lead in AI advancements, there's a significant "AI divide" growing between these nations and the rest of the world. This division risks creating a new form of inequality on the global stage, where countries with AI capabilities can exert disproportionate influence over those without.

Moreover, the militarization of AI is a growing concern. From autonomous drones to cyber warfare algorithms, AI has the potential to revolutionize how conflicts are fought. This not only raises ethical questions but also poses risks of accidental escalations, where an AI error could potentially lead to catastrophic consequences.

Therefore, international frameworks for AI governance, akin to existing treaties on nuclear proliferation or climate change, are increasingly becoming a necessity. Such agreements could set guidelines on ethical practices, data sharing, and even restrict the militarization of AI, thus preventing an "AI arms race."

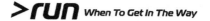
Chapter 8: AI in the Arts

The Dawn of a New Creative Era

For as long as human history goes back, the arts have been a fundamental part of our experience. From the earliest cave paintings to modern multimedia installations, art has been a way to express our thoughts, feelings, and perceptions. Now, we are at a critical juncture where technology, particularly artificial intelligence, is merging with artistic creation. What does this marriage mean for the arts, and how does it redefine the boundaries of creativity?

From Music Generation to Art Creation

When it comes to music, artificial intelligence is already showing its prowess. Algorithms, with the help of machine learning, can compose scores in multiple genres, creating everything from symphonies to pop hits. In an industry that often struggles with creative blocks and financial limitations, AI offers a new set of tools for composers and musicians. Companies like AIVA and initiatives like Google's Magenta are pioneering this space, making AI-composed music not just a theoretical venture but a growing commercial reality.

However, the entry of AI into the creative musical landscape isn't without its controversies. While AI tools can serve as aides for professional musicians and composers, they also risk commodifying the creative process. When an algorithm can churn out a pop hit in a matter of minutes, it inevitably raises questions about the originality, ownership, and the very essence of creativity.

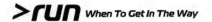

The Transformation of Visual Arts

AI's role is not limited to the auditory arts; it is making significant strides in visual arts as well. From algorithmically generated paintings to AI-curated exhibitions, technology is revolutionizing how we create and consume visual art. Companies like DeepArt and tools like Google's DeepDream offer artists and even ordinary individuals the chance to create intricate pieces without having a background in fine arts. These platforms use neural networks to understand and apply artistic styles, thereby democratizing the act of creation.

Yet, this democratization comes with its challenges, notably surrounding the topic of authenticity. If anyone can create a piece of art with the help of an algorithm, does it dilute the value of artistic skill? Furthermore, how does one determine the ownership of these creations? These questions are further complicated when algorithms autonomously create art, pushing us to reconsider our definitions of authorship and originality.

Authenticity and Creativity

The dialogue about AI and the arts invariably lands on the topic of authenticity. What does it mean for a piece of art to be 'authentic' in the age of AI? Historically, we've held the belief that art is an individual's creative expression, a singular vision brought to life through skill and inspiration. AI, however, complicates this perception. When a machine generates art, questions surrounding its authenticity naturally arise.

These questions extend to the realm of copyrights and intellectual property as well. Should an AI-generated piece of art be copyrighted, and if so, who holds that right? Is it the individual who programmed the algorithm, the user who utilized the tool, or does the AI itself have some claim to ownership? Legal systems worldwide are grappling with these unprecedented issues, and it's likely to be a long journey before we arrive at conclusive answers.

The Audience's Role

The integration of AI into the arts also changes the role of the audience. In conventional settings, the audience is a consumer of the artistic creation. In contrast, AI makes the viewer an active participant. Take, for instance, interactive AI installations that adapt in real-time to the audience's reactions. Such setups challenge our traditional notions of authorship and ownership, adding layers of complexity to how we define art.

Imagine a digital art installation that morphs based on the emotional reactions of its viewers, captured through real-time facial recognition or other biometric data. This not only makes the artwork more interactive but also challenges the dichotomy between the creator and the consumer. The line separating the two becomes increasingly blurred, making each piece a collective work of art.

Ethical Implications in AI-Generated Art

As with any domain where AI gains prominence, ethical considerations in AI-generated art are of paramount importance. For one, there is the concern of cultural appropriation. Algorithms don't understand the cultural significance behind specific styles or symbols; they replicate them based on the data they're trained on. This can lead to inadvertent but damaging misrepresentations.

Moreover, the use of personal data in interactive art forms requires strict guidelines. If an installation is capturing facial reactions or other biometric data, the question of data privacy comes into play. How is this data stored, and who has access to it? These ethical dimensions necessitate stringent guidelines, combining the expertise of tech developers, artists, and policymakers.

The Economic Perspective

As AI tools become more accessible, they are also likely to impact the economics of the art world. For many artists, AI can serve as a powerful assistant, reducing the time and effort required to create complex pieces. However, the flip side is the potential for job displacement. If algorithms can produce art more quickly and perhaps more cheaply, what happens to professional artists? This creates an urgency for redefining artistic value in an AI-driven world, ensuring that technology serves as an enabler rather than a disruptor.

AI and Literature

The influence of AI isn't confined to visual and auditory arts; it's permeating the literary world as well. AI algorithms have been developed to write poetry, short stories, and even entire novels. While these may not yet match the depth and complexity of human-created literature, the rapid advancements in natural language processing indicate that AI-written literature could become more sophisticated in the near future.

Once again, this poses questions about originality and authenticity. If an AI can write a novel or a poem, how do we judge its literary value? Unlike human authors, algorithms lack personal experiences or emotional depth. Therefore, the 'why' behind each written word is purely a calculation, devoid of any emotional undertone, challenging our traditional criteria for assessing literary quality.

As we delve deeper into the intersections of AI and art, it's crucial to maintain an ongoing dialogue about the ethical, social, and philosophical implications. This isn't merely a technological evolution; it's a cultural revolution, reshaping how we create, consume, and think about art. With AI's continued advancement, we stand on the brink of a transformative era in human creativity, filled with unimaginable possibilities and complex challenges.

The Role of Algorithms in Artistic Endeavors

To understand the influence of AI in the art world, we must first delve into the algorithms that make this possible. Algorithms in AI-driven artistic platforms usually employ deep learning techniques. These deep neural networks are trained on vast amounts of data—paintings, music compositions, poems, etc —to recognize patterns, styles, and techniques. Once trained, these networks can generate new pieces that incorporate learned elements.

The technology itself is agnostic about art forms. Whether it's visual arts like painting and photography, or auditory arts like music, or even literary arts like poetry and storytelling, deep learning algorithms can cater to a broad range of artistic pursuits. The versatility of AI algorithms means that the boundary between traditional human creativity and machine-generated art is becoming increasingly blurred.

But the adaptability of AI in artistic platforms also raises questions. For example, if a machine can be trained to compose a sonnet in the style of Shakespeare or paint in the brushstrokes of Van Gogh, does that diminish the value of original works by these artists? This leads to discussions on the cultural and philosophical ramifications of AI in arts, topics that are by no means settled but are certainly the subject of vigorous debate.

AI and the Future of Collaborative Art

The influence of AI doesn't stop at individual art creation; it also extends to collaborative projects. For example, there are platforms where AI algorithms work in tandem with human artists, suggesting improvements, alternative techniques, or even entirely new concepts. This kind of AI-human collaboration opens up new avenues for innovation in the art world.

The future might witness large-scale collaborative projects involving multiple artists and AI algorithms working in harmony. Imagine a monumental painting or a musical symphony crafted not just by human hands but aided by the computational power of AI. The possibilities are almost limitless, yet they also warrant caution. When many contributors—both human and machine—are involved, questions about authorship, rights, and intellectual property become even more complicated.

Audience's Role in AI Art

The relationship between the artist and the audience changes in an AI-augmented artistic landscape. Traditional arts often involve a one-way communication channel from the artist to the audience. However, with AI in the equation, this dynamic shifts. AI-generated or AI-assisted art often incorporates feedback loops, where audience reactions and preferences can be collected and analyzed to influence future creations.

This sort of dynamic art could usher in a new form of participatory art, where the audience is not just a passive consumer but an active contributor. It adds an extra layer of complexity and interactivity to the art world, which some may find exciting and others disconcerting. Either way, the role of the audience is undergoing a transformation, and the ramifications of this change are still being understood.

Practical Considerations and Ethical Implications

The use of AI in arts also brings along a slew of practical considerations. Licensing and copyright laws were designed with human creators in mind and are ill-equipped to handle creations partially or wholly generated by machines. Who owns the copyright to a piece of AI-generated art? Is it the developer who created the algorithm, the user who executed it, or a joint ownership between the two? These questions have yet to be conclusively answered, adding another layer of complexity to the already intricate landscape of AI in arts.

Then there are the ethical considerations. The use of AI to replicate or imitate the styles of existing or late artists raises ethical questions about authenticity and respect for original works. The possibility of AI-generated fake art entering the market poses serious challenges for the art community and buyers alike. Moreover, the use of AI in art also stirs debates about cultural appropriation, especially when algorithms are trained on art forms originating from specific ethnic or social groups.

AI in Art Education

Beyond the professional art world, AI also has a significant role to play in art education. Educational institutions and online platforms are increasingly integrating AI tools into their curricula to aid in teaching various art forms. From algorithms that can critique a student's painting in real-time to systems that can identify areas of improvement in a musical composition, AI is making art education more interactive and personalized.

Teachers and students alike find value in these AI-augmented educational tools. For instructors, AI can handle the more mundane aspects of teaching, like grading or basic feedback, freeing them to focus on more complex nuanced aspects of art. For students, AI provides a new avenue for immediate, personalized feedback, allowing them to improve rapidly without waiting for scheduled critique sessions.

However, the rise of AI in art education also introduces several challenges. One obvious concern is that students might become overly reliant on AI tools, thereby losing the capacity for independent critical thinking and creativity. There's also the risk that the algorithms might introduce or perpetuate biases, based on the data they've been trained on, impacting the way art is taught and evaluated.

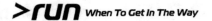

Monetization and Market Transformation

The penetration of AI into the art world is also transforming the market dynamics. AI-generated art pieces are gradually finding their place in galleries, exhibitions, and online marketplaces. Some have even fetched hefty sums in auctions, putting them in the same league as works created by human artists. This is a double-edged sword. On one hand, it provides a new revenue stream for artists who can master the use of AI tools. On the other, it risks saturating the market with mass-produced art, potentially devaluing individual creativity.

The impact extends to art dealers, galleries, and collectors as well. With AI-generated art becoming more accessible, the barriers to entry in the art market are lowered. This democratization allows more people to participate in art creation and consumption but also leads to challenges in art valuation, authenticity, and provenance.

Ethical Dimensions Revisited

As AI takes on a more prominent role in the art world, ethical considerations continue to evolve. There's a growing call for transparency in how algorithms are trained and deployed in art creation. Transparent practices can help address several ethical issues, such as bias, authenticity, and ownership, making the integration of AI into the art world more responsible and ethical.

Transparency is not just a technical requirement but also an ethical imperative. It allows for more inclusive decision-making processes, involving artists, technologists, and even the audience in discussions that shape the future of AI in art. This collective decision-making can help ensure that AI is used in a manner that respects the artistic process and the sanctity of individual creativity, instead of undermining it.

AI Curation in Museums and Exhibitions

Another fascinating aspect of AI's influence on the art world is its role in curating exhibitions. Algorithms are being developed to analyze numerous variables like historical relevance, artistic styles, and public interest to suggest the best possible configurations for exhibitions. AI systems can also help identify emerging trends and overlooked pieces of art that deserve more attention, making curation a more dynamic and democratic process.

However, the role of AI in curation raises questions about the expertise and intuition that human curators bring to the table. AI might be capable of pattern recognition and data analysis, but it lacks the nuanced understanding of art's emotional and cultural impact, at least as of now. Can an algorithm truly understand the context behind a piece of art the way a human can?

Virtual Reality and AI: A New Canvas

Virtual Reality (VR) combined with AI is creating an entirely new platform for artists to express themselves. Artists are using VR tools that incorporate AI algorithms to craft immersive experiences unlike anything possible on a two-dimensional plane. This amalgamation of technology and art opens up possibilities for interactive art installations, where the AI algorithm responds to viewers' movements, choices, or even emotional expressions, creating a dynamic piece of art that evolves over time.

Yet, this integration of VR and AI also prompts a discussion on accessibility. High-quality VR setups are often expensive and not readily available to the average consumer, creating a potential divide between those who can experience this new form of art and those who cannot.

Criticisms and Controversies

As with any disruptive technology, AI's foray into the art world has its share of critics and controversies. Critics argue that the use of AI diminishes the value of human skill and creativity, reducing art to mere algorithms and data points. There is also ongoing debate about the ownership and copyright issues surrounding AI-generated art. Who owns the rights to an art piece created with the aid of AI? Is it the programmer who designed the algorithm, the artist who used the tool, or a combination of both?

These questions add another layer of complexity to the already intricate world of art law and ethics. They force us to reconsider the very definitions of artistry, creativity, and ownership, as technology continues to blur the traditional boundaries.

Intellectual Property and the Uncanny Valley of Art

In a rapidly evolving landscape, intellectual property concerns have come to the forefront. Given that AI-generated art is a blend of human input and algorithmic creation, existing copyright laws face challenges in determining the rightful owner of the artwork. Furthermore, algorithms can produce pieces that are eerily similar to existing human-made art, which raises issues of plagiarism and originality. This leads to the "uncanny valley" of art, where AI-generated pieces can be so lifelike or similar to human-produced pieces that it becomes disconcerting. How do we navigate these intricate issues without stifling creativity and innovation?

The Audience's Evolving Role

Audiences are no longer mere spectators but active participants in the creation and interpretation of art, thanks to AI. With interactive exhibitions, social media shares, and even algorithms that adapt an art piece based on viewer engagement, the role of the audience has never been more central. However, this democratization comes with its set of challenges. For one, the sanctity and original vision of the artwork can be compromised. Secondly, the traditional roles of artist, curator, and spectator become muddled, raising questions about authorship and the integrity of the art world.

Artists' Perspective: A Tool or a Threat?

Many artists view AI as an extension of the palette, a tool that augments their ability to create. Others, however, see AI as an existential threat that could diminish the value of human creativity. So, what does this schism mean for the future of art? Could there be a synthesis of both views, or are we heading toward a bifurcation in the art world, one that separates 'pure' human art from that which is machine-assisted or machine-generated?

Machine Learning and the Preservation of Art

In addition to its role in creation, AI is being used in the preservation of art. Machine learning algorithms can analyze the condition of artworks and suggest appropriate restoration methods. For cultural artifacts and aging masterpieces, this could extend their lifespans and make them accessible to future generations. Yet, this technological intervention could also alter the very essence of these works, as minor changes and restorations could affect their historical and cultural value.

AI's Role in Artistic Collaboration and Experimentation

The concept of artistic collaboration has undergone significant transformation with the advent of AI. Previously limited to human-to-human interaction, collaborations can now take place between artists and AI algorithms. This has opened up new avenues for experimentation and has fundamentally changed how we think about partnerships in the creative process.

In a collaboration with AI, the artist's expertise in themes, composition, and expression melds with the machine's capability to generate endless variations, analyze vast datasets, and even predict audience reactions. This symbiotic relationship can lead to art that transcends traditional limitations, offering a richer, more varied creative output.

However, this new form of collaboration also leads to several challenges, such as determining authorship and assessing the 'soul' or emotional resonance of the artwork. It brings up issues of credibility—do we view an art piece generated with AI assistance as 'lesser' than one made entirely by human hands? Is the artist merely a 'curator' of the machine's output, or do they remain the primary creative force?

The Aesthetics of AI in Art

As AI becomes increasingly involved in the art world, its influence has given rise to a new aesthetic discourse. What are the specific aesthetics of AI-generated or AI-assisted art? To what extent do they differ from those associated with human-made creations?

One remarkable point of divergence is the ability of AI to produce artworks in mass quantities, a feature that artists are leveraging for broader experimentation and discovery of new aesthetic realms. However, this vast output capability poses its own ethical questions. When AI can create thousands of iterations in a matter of seconds, what does this mean for the unique, 'one-of-a-kind' value that we traditionally ascribe to art? How does this change the economy of art, especially when it comes to pricing and exclusivity?

Moreover, with AI, artists can now explore previously impossible forms, patterns, and even entire artistic languages. Advanced 3D modeling, intricate fractals, and mind-bending visual effects can be produced more easily. However, some critics argue that this could dilute the skill set traditionally associated with artistic endeavor. Does mastery of the brush hold the same value when an algorithm can simulate its effect in a digital format? How will this shift in aesthetics affect art education and appreciation?

AI and the Democratization of Art

The use of AI in art extends beyond the realm of professional artists and into the broader public. User-friendly software and applications equipped with AI algorithms are enabling people with minimal artistic training to create complex artworks. This raises the question of democratization in the art world. Could AI be the great equalizer, leveling the playing field between trained artists and amateurs? Or does it further widen the gap by providing another tool that only the economically privileged can access?

These platforms are pushing the boundaries of what we consider 'art' and 'artist.' Social media platforms are flooded with AI-generated art pieces, be it a filter applied to a photograph or a full-fledged digital painting. This phenomenon has triggered an ongoing debate about the dilution of artistic quality. With the barrier to entry significantly lowered, what measures can be taken to maintain the integrity of art as a discipline?

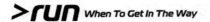

However, the democratization effect has its upside. For one, it allows for the uncovering of latent talent, providing opportunities to those who might not have had access to formal artistic education or resources. It's an inclusive move, one that can diversify the art world in terms of both creators and audiences.

Ethical Considerations in AI and Art

As AI continues to find its way into the artistic realm, it raises a plethora of ethical considerations that both creators and consumers must ponder. Questions of ownership, copyright, and intellectual property rights become murky when machine learning algorithms have a hand in generating artworks. How do we fairly distribute recognition and compensation in such collaborative endeavors?

Moreover, the influence of AI in art extends beyond mere production; it is also shaping consumption and criticism. Algorithms on social media platforms, art websites, and virtual galleries can affect what art gets seen, appreciated, and eventually purchased. This algorithmic curation could perpetuate biases and limit diversity within the art world. What steps must be taken to ensure that AI does not skew the artistic landscape toward a homogenized, monolithic culture?

One cannot ignore the ethical implications tied to the data used in training AI for artistic purposes. This data often includes art pieces, styles, and techniques from a range of cultural backgrounds. As such, concerns about cultural appropriation arise, especially when the AI-generated artwork does not appropriately credit or respect the origins of its influences. When using machine learning algorithms trained on a global dataset, how can artists ensure they are not inadvertently participating in cultural erasure or misrepresentation?

Lastly, the sustainability aspect of AI in art is also an issue that cannot be swept under the rug. The computational power required to run complex algorithms is energy-intensive and contributes to environmental concerns. As artists and developers, there is a responsibility to be conscious of the carbon footprint generated in the creation of AI-assisted artworks. Are there ways to offset this impact, and how can we develop more eco-friendly technologies moving forward?

The Future of AI in Art: An Intersection of Possibilities and Challenges

As we look toward the future, it's clear that the intersection of AI and art will continue to evolve in ways that are both exciting and unpredictable. New technologies are constantly emerging, each with the potential to redefine the boundaries of artistic endeavor. Yet, as is often the case with disruptive innovations, these developments will present their own sets of ethical, aesthetic, and socio-economic challenges that society must grapple with.

For instance, as AI technology becomes more accessible, we may see a surge in the number of 'AI artists,' individuals or entities that solely rely on machine learning algorithms for the creation of artworks. While this could expand the realm of what we consider art, it also risks saturating the market with works that lack the emotional depth and nuance that come from human experience and interpretation. Can we find a balance between technological prowess and emotional resonance?

Furthermore, as AI becomes increasingly sophisticated, the lines between human-generated and machine-generated art will continue to blur. This could lead to contentious debates around authenticity, with potential ramifications for art markets, galleries, and even legal frameworks around copyright and ownership. How will we adapt existing institutions and norms to accommodate this evolving landscape?

In the grand scheme of things, the integration of AI into the art world presents both an exciting frontier and a complex maze of challenges that artists, technologists, and society at large will have to navigate. As we move forward, it is essential that we engage in multidisciplinary dialogues to explore this intersection in a thoughtful, ethical, and inclusive manner. By doing so, we can ensure that the union of AI and art enriches our culture rather than impoverishing it.

The Economics of AI in Art

While it's clear that AI's role in the art world brings a range of ethical and aesthetic considerations to the forefront, its economic impact is equally significant and warrants dedicated exploration. How does the advent of AI technology affect the valuation of artworks? How is the traditional art market adapting or resisting this technological disruption?

The notion of value in art has always been subject to a myriad of influences, from the artist's reputation to the medium's exclusivity, from historical context to sheer public opinion. With AI entering the scene, we must also factor in the cost of the technology itself, including the data storage and computational power required for AI algorithms. Moreover, AI's democratizing effect, which allows more individuals to produce art with the help of algorithms, can dilute the market and potentially depress the prices of artworks. While this makes art more accessible, it poses challenges to traditional valuation models.

Marketplaces for AI-generated art have sprouted up online, fostering an ecosystem that functions outside traditional gallery and auction house systems. Such platforms often use blockchain technology to verify the uniqueness and ownership of digital artworks. This innovation, however, poses its own challenges. For one, the decentralized nature of blockchain markets can make it more difficult for artists and collectors to navigate legal channels in cases of copyright infringement or disputes over provenance. How will the economic systems surrounding art adapt to these rapid changes?

Perhaps one of the most significant economic considerations is the distribution of profits in cases where artworks are produced collaboratively between humans and AI. As of now, there's no industry standard for how revenue from such works should be divided. Should the developers of the AI algorithm receive a percentage? What about the individuals who contributed to the data on which the AI was trained? The resolution of these questions will have a lasting impact on how artists, technologists, and consumers interact within this evolving market.

In summary, AI's involvement in the art world isn't merely an aesthetic or ethical concern; it has broad economic ramifications that are already shaking up traditional systems of value, ownership, and profit. For artists and collectors navigating this landscape, adaptability and a deep understanding of both technology and market trends are becoming increasingly crucial.

AI-Driven Storytelling

AI-generated content is gaining traction, not only in the realm of news and journalism but also in fiction and storytelling. This is yet another testament to how the lines between human-generated and machine-generated content are increasingly blurred. Companies like OpenAI have developed text-generating models, capable of creating entire articles, stories, and even poetry, in response to simple prompts.

The AI storytelling platforms are not a simple, mindless reproduction of existing content. They operate on intricate algorithms that can analyze existing literature, pick up on styles, and even adopt the 'voice' of specific writers. The machine isn't only spitting out words; it's offering an interpretation of the literary world it has 'studied.'

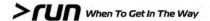

That brings us to the question: Are AI-created stories art? And if they are, what does that mean for human authors and creators? Some argue that since AI lacks the emotional intelligence and life experiences that human writers bring to the table, its creations can never be considered true art. Others counter that AI can imitate human style so well that the end reader can't distinguish the source. These two perspectives bring the art world into a quandary, grappling with the notion of authenticity in the digital age.

The Audience's Role

The debate around the place of AI in the arts often overlooks the role of the audience or the consumer. In traditional art forms, the audience plays a pivotal role in attributing value to the artwork. The interpretation of a painting, the emotional reaction to a music piece, or the critical reception of a book—these are all factors that contribute to the 'worth' of a piece of art.

AI's involvement complicates this dynamic. For example, if an AI algorithm generates a piece of music based on your previous listening history and mood, you might find it highly appealing. Here, the machine has directly interacted with your personal preference, perhaps even more intimately than a human artist might. But does that interaction elevate the AI-generated music to the status of art?

The audience's role is increasingly becoming a part of the creation process itself, facilitated by machine learning algorithms. Algorithms can adapt and fine-tune their outputs based on user interaction and feedback, thereby offering a unique, personalized art experience. This active participation of the audience in the creative process opens up a new frontier in the definition and valuation of art.

AI as a Collaborative Tool for Artists

As AI evolves, its potential as a tool for human artists is also expanding. Tools like DALL-E for visual art or Jukebox for music are becoming collaborative platforms. Artists are using these technologies to generate initial drafts or concepts, which they then refine and build upon. In a way, AI acts as a creative partner, offering ideas that the artist might not have conceived otherwise.

This collaboration doesn't just stop at individual artists. AI is starting to penetrate the world of collaborative art projects that involve multiple human participants. Algorithms can synchronize the creative inputs of various artists, offering a cohesive final product that reflects a blend of multiple styles and ideas. This could potentially revolutionize collaborative art forms like theatre, orchestral music, or mural painting, where synchronization and cohesion are vital.

The Ethics of AI in Art

When we bring AI into the realm of the arts, ethical considerations naturally follow. If an AI model generates a painting that closely resembles the style of a famous artist, is it an original work, or is it plagiarism? Furthermore, who owns the rights to AI-generated art? The programmer who designed the algorithm? The user who provided the initial prompt? Or does nobody own it, given that the 'creator' is a machine?

These questions have yet to be answered definitively, leading to a nebulous area where legality, ethics, and art intersect. There's also the question of monetization. As AI-generated art becomes more prevalent, it poses a potential threat to human artists in terms of competition for attention and resources.

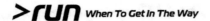

To navigate this complex landscape, some organizations and artists are advocating for a clearer legal framework around AI-generated art. This would include guidelines on intellectual property, recognition, and even revenue-sharing models that ensure human artists aren't sidelined as machines become more adept at creative tasks.

AI's role in the arts is a fascinating, complex subject that raises questions about creativity, authenticity, and value. It's a topic that not only impacts artists but also has far-reaching implications for society as a whole. As we continue to navigate the confluence of technology and creativity, it's crucial to establish ethical and practical guidelines that honor both human innovation and machine capabilities.

AI's Impact on Cultural Preservation

Another area worth discussing is AI's role in cultural preservation, particularly in the arts. Many traditional art forms are at risk of disappearing as older generations pass away without passing on their knowledge and skills. Artificial intelligence offers a way to capture, digitize, and preserve these fading art forms for future generations.

For example, AI can be trained to recognize and catalog various forms of traditional dance, music, or painting styles. It can analyze nuances in performance techniques, offering a comprehensive digital archive. This ensures that even if the last practitioners of a particular art form pass away, the art form itself may continue to live in the digital realm. Here again, we see the paradox of machine learning 'capturing' human creativity for the sake of preservation, potentially freezing it in time rather than allowing it to evolve naturally.

AI and Art Education

Art education is undergoing a transformation with the integration of AI technologies. Not only can AI help with administrative tasks, freeing up educators to focus more on actual teaching, but it can also personalize learning experiences for students. An AI-driven system can analyze a student's performance and tailor subsequent lessons according to individual weaknesses and strengths.

For art students, this is a game-changer. AI could offer real-time feedback during a drawing exercise, suggest different painting techniques based on the style the student is aiming for, or even propose new compositions for a music student. It's like having a personal tutor who understands your unique learning style and offers relevant guidance.

The concept of AI in education also brings us back to the notion of 'learning.' If machines can 'teach,' what does this mean for human educators? This is an ongoing debate in the field of educational technology and one that intersects with our larger discussion on AI and the arts.

Personalization vs. Homogenization

A potentially unintended consequence of using AI in the arts is the risk of homogenization. As algorithms get better at predicting what people like, there's a danger that they'll keep feeding us more of the same, thus narrowing our exposure and reducing diversity in art forms. It's the algorithmic equivalent of an 'echo chamber,' where your pre-existing preferences are reinforced, limiting exposure to new and different forms of art.

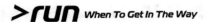

However, some argue that AI, if programmed with this concern in mind, can actually be used to combat homogenization. Algorithms can be designed to introduce 'randomness' or 'surprises'—suggesting art forms, music genres, or literature that a person wouldn't ordinarily encounter. This could help broaden horizons and promote diversity in the arts, counteracting the very issue it could potentially exacerbate.

AI in Art Curation and the Museum Experience

In recent years, museums and art galleries have begun embracing AI to enhance the visitor experience. These institutions traditionally serve as custodians of culture, art, and history. Still, they are increasingly becoming intersections where technology meets art. One exciting development is the use of AI to personalize art curation.

Visitors can now use AI-driven applications on their smartphones that analyze individual preferences, learning from what art pieces or historical artifacts engage them the most. This personal curation is revolutionary. Imagine walking through the Louvre, and your app directs you to Mona Lisa but also suggests lesser-known artworks based on your prior interest in Renaissance art. Such technology not only enriches the visitor's experience but also allows lesser-known artworks to receive attention.

Moreover, AI can also handle logistics and visitor flow within these spaces. Crowd management is a significant concern for popular exhibitions. AI algorithms can predict and manage visitor numbers by analyzing data such as ticket sales, seasonal trends, and even social media buzz, helping institutions to allocate resources more efficiently.

AI's Role in Art Preservation and Restoration

Another noteworthy contribution of AI is in the realm of art preservation and restoration. With time, art pieces suffer from wear and tear, environmental conditions, or even vandalism. Restoring them is a delicate, often expensive, process requiring a high level of expertise. AI can aid human experts in this endeavor by providing precise analyses of an artwork's condition, comparing it to a database of the artist's other works or a similar style or period. This can result in more accurate restoration, saving countless invaluable works for future generations.

In 2018, a project involving AI was instrumental in restoring a series of damaged frescoes in an ancient Roman villa. The AI was trained on images of well-preserved frescoes and then applied this knowledge to digitally restore the damaged parts, providing restorers with a detailed guide for their work. This shows that AI doesn't replace human skill but augments it, offering tools that can lead to better, more informed decisions.

Ethical Questions in AI's Involvement in Art

However, AI's involvement in the arts isn't devoid of controversies. For instance, when AI is used to create art, who owns the copyright? Is it the programmer, the operator of the AI, or the AI itself? As of now, the law is ill-equipped to answer these questions, leaving a gray area that is open to interpretation and disputes.

Another concern is the potential for AI to perpetuate existing biases in the art world. Just like in other sectors, the data used to train these AIs could be biased, reflecting historical gender, racial, or cultural biases. If not checked, there's a risk that these AIs will amplify these biases, further marginalizing underrepresented artists and art forms.

Despite these challenges, it is undeniable that AI has opened up new horizons in the arts, both for creators and audiences. As we move forward, it's crucial to engage in open dialogues about the ethical implications and to refine the technology responsibly.

We are at a junction where art and technology are becoming increasingly interdependent, with each enriching the other in unexpected ways. AI's influence on the arts is not just a transient trend but a paradigm shift that holds the promise of a more inclusive, interactive, and enriched artistic landscape.

Let's not forget that the ultimate goal of both art and technology is to enrich the human experience. If balanced correctly, the symbiotic relationship between AI and art can take us closer to achieving this lofty aim. Artists, technologists, and policymakers must work together to ensure that this collaboration serves to uplift, inspire, and challenge us, just as great art has always done.

The role of AI in the arts is not just transformative from a creative standpoint but also from an economic perspective. The technology has the potential to significantly affect the art market, from pricing and valuation to distribution and accessibility.

In traditional art auctions, for example, the value of a piece is determined by various factors, such as the artist's reputation, the work's condition, its provenance, and subjective judgments about its quality or importance. AI can analyze these data points on a large scale, enabling more accurate valuations. Automated valuation models, or AVMs, are being used in some art markets to provide instant, data-backed appraisals.

The implications of this go beyond individual sales. Insurance companies, galleries, and museums can use this data to assess their collections' value and make data-informed decisions about acquisitions, sales, and exhibits. Furthermore, AI can democratize art by opening up smaller markets and giving emerging artists a chance to be seen and valued objectively, based on the merit of their work rather than their connections in the art world.

AI and Art Education

Traditionally, art education has relied on human experts—artists, historians, and teachers—to impart knowledge and skills. With AI, we are beginning to see a shift towards a more democratized form of education in the arts. From AI tutors that can provide instant feedback on an art project to algorithms that can sort through thousands of artworks and provide a curated educational experience, the potential applications are boundless.

Online courses can now include interactive, AI-driven components that adapt to a student's learning pace and preferences. These adaptive learning platforms can also serve as a supplementary tool for educators, freeing them from administrative tasks and allowing them to focus more on fostering creativity and critical thinking.

AI in Art Therapy and Mental Health

Another less discussed but equally crucial aspect of AI in art is its therapeutic potential. Art therapy is a well-established field that uses the creative process to help people explore their emotions, improve self-esteem, manage addictions, relieve stress, and improve symptoms of anxiety and depression. Although the human element will always be central to therapy, AI can offer new tools and approaches to treatment.

For instance, AI algorithms can analyze artwork created in therapy sessions to detect patterns or changes over time, providing valuable insights into a patient's emotional state and progress. This is not to say that AI could replace human therapists, but rather it could serve as a powerful adjunct, providing data that can help guide treatment plans.

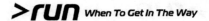

Challenges and Limitations

While the prospects of AI in the arts are exciting, there are also challenges and limitations to consider. One significant concern is the fear that AI could replace human artists or curators. However, it's essential to note that AI tools are just that—tools. They don't possess the emotional intelligence, cultural context, or creative intuition that human artists do.

Therefore, the challenge lies in finding the right balance between human creativity and AI's capabilities. This balance could vary significantly depending on the art form and the individual artist's preferences and needs. But as we move forward, it's critical that we don't lose sight of what makes art fundamentally human: its ability to inspire, provoke, and connect us in ways that nothing else can.

Chapter 9: AI Ethics in the Realm of Art

Introduction

Art, as a form of human expression, has always been subject to ethical considerations, whether it's the depiction of religious figures, the use of certain materials, or the cultural appropriation of styles and techniques. In the age of artificial intelligence, these ethical questions take on new dimensions. This chapter aims to explore the moral implications and challenges that arise as AI technologies make their way into the world of art. It will delve into issues related to creative ownership, potential biases in AI algorithms, and the ethical considerations of AI in art education and therapy.

Ownership and Copyright Issues

One of the most pressing ethical issues concerning the integration of AI into the art world is that of ownership and copyright. When an AI creates a piece of art, who owns it? The programmer who coded the algorithm? The user who inputted the data or provided the parameters for the art to be generated? Or does nobody own it because the art was not produced by a human?

To address these questions, we must re-evaluate what we consider as "creative labor." Historically, copyright laws have focused on human endeavor, ignoring or dismissing the creative output of machines. However, as AI systems become more sophisticated and autonomous, this position is increasingly untenable.

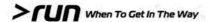

Furthermore, the "mash-up" culture prevalent on platforms like Instagram and TikTok complicates matters. In this setting, AI-generated artworks could be modified, remixed, and shared widely, often without the original creator's knowledge or consent. Legal frameworks have been slow to catch up with these rapid developments, leaving artists, programmers, and consumers in a murky ethical landscape.

Bias and Representation

Another ethical challenge in employing AI in art is the issue of bias. AI algorithms are trained on existing datasets, and if those datasets include historical or societal biases, the AI will inevitably perpetuate them. For instance, if an AI program is trained solely on Western art, it might not generate art that represents other cultures accurately, or it may reinforce stereotypes.

Even in abstract art, algorithmic biases could affect the color palette, forms, and structures that the AI chooses, inadvertently shaping the viewer's perceptions and emotional reactions. This form of bias, though more subtle, could still perpetuate a narrow view of what art should be, thereby excluding entire communities and cultures from the artistic conversation.

Ethical Implications in Art Education and Therapy

As AI becomes an integral part of art education and therapy, it's crucial to consider its ethical implications. Algorithms could replace human educators in assessing student work, offering critiques, and even suggesting improvements. While this may democratize access to quality art education, it could also stifle creative freedom and impose a standardized, algorithmically determined notion of "good art."

In the realm of art therapy, the use of AI could raise concerns about privacy and emotional safety. For instance, if an AI algorithm analyses the artworks produced in therapy sessions to assess a patient's mental state, who gets to see that data? And how secure is it?

Ethical Guidelines and Future Directions

Given these challenges, it's essential for stakeholders in art and technology to collaborate in developing ethical guidelines. These should address issues ranging from creative ownership and copyright to the prevention of algorithmic bias. Just as art has its own ethical frameworks—ranging from plagiarism to the responsible depiction of sensitive subjects—so too should the intersection of AI and art.

As we move forward into an increasingly digital and automated future, it's crucial to ask these ethical questions. If the art world is to embrace AI, it must do so responsibly, ensuring that we enhance creative expression rather than restrict it, and that we extend the benefits of AI-driven art to all, rather than a privileged few.

The Ethical Implications of Deepfakes in Art

The rise of deepfake technology poses another set of ethical concerns in the realm of art. Deepfakes, created through deep learning algorithms, are convincing fake videos or images that superimpose existing footage or photos. The ethical ramifications are manifold. From the creation of counterfeit artworks to the manipulation of an artist's original work in a way that could damage their reputation, the potential for misuse is substantial.

The art world has already seen instances of deepfake technology being used to create counterfeit artworks sold as originals. In a similar vein, deepfakes could be used to create 'new' works by deceased artists, leading to ethical and legal questions about ownership and legacy. Moreover, deepfake technology has the potential to disrupt the trust in the digital art market, which has gained significant traction in recent years through the advent of NFTs (Non-Fungible Tokens).

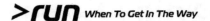

On the flip side, deepfake technology presents artists with powerful new tools for creative expression. Artists have already begun experimenting with deepfakes as a medium, raising questions about authenticity and the value of 'original' art. However, like any powerful tool, the ethical implications must be considered carefully, necessitating a framework that delineates acceptable from unacceptable uses.

The Role of Galleries and Curators

With the increasing digitization of art, galleries and curators also have an ethical responsibility in the new landscape shaped by AI. Traditionally, the role of galleries and curators has been to select, interpret, and present art to the public. This involves making numerous ethical decisions, such as which artists to represent, how to price artworks, and how to describe and display them.

In a world where AI-generated art becomes more prevalent, galleries and curators must consider the implications of showcasing such works. For instance, should AI-created art be labeled explicitly to distinguish it from human-created art? And how should galleries deal with the aforementioned issues of copyright and ownership?

Additionally, galleries and museums often serve an educational role. This function becomes especially crucial as the public navigates the new complexities introduced by AI in art. Galleries must decide how to educate their audiences about the technology behind the art, the ethical considerations involved, and the broader societal implications.

Artists, AI, and Moral Responsibility

Artists who choose to incorporate AI into their practice also take on additional ethical responsibilities. Unlike traditional forms of art, AI-generated art often involves collaboration with technologists and scientists. As artists make choices about which algorithms to use or what data to train their AI on, they make ethical decisions that have ramifications beyond their personal artistic vision.

For example, if an artist chooses to use an AI trained on a dataset of classical European art, they risk perpetuating Eurocentric perspectives and biases. This becomes an ethical issue, particularly if the artist is unaware of or indifferent to the biases inherent in their chosen algorithm. Furthermore, if artists make use of data that isn't publicly available or violates copyright or privacy norms, they run the risk of ethical and legal repercussions.

Artists, therefore, need to be as transparent as possible about their methods and choices when creating AI-generated art. This could range from disclosing the datasets and algorithms used, to actively seeking out and employing more diverse and inclusive datasets in their work.

As we navigate this unprecedented era of AI integration into art, ethics must be at the forefront of the discussion. From questions of ownership and copyright to the challenges posed by algorithmic bias and deepfake technology, there is a critical need for clear ethical guidelines. Artists, curators, galleries, technologists, and policymakers must engage in a multidisciplinary dialogue to address these issues comprehensively.

By proactively tackling these ethical considerations, we can hope to guide the development of AI in art in a direction that enriches human creativity and broadens our understanding of what art can be, while respecting and preserving the ethical principles that have long guided artistic endeavor.

Surveillance and National Security

While the potential for autonomous weapons in warfare is one aspect, AI has another, less talked about, but equally significant role—surveillance and national security. The vast data troves generated by citizens and infrastructure are rich grounds for AI algorithms. These data can be used for various purposes, from tracking potential terrorist activities to monitoring international communications.

However, the use of AI for national security is not without its ethical considerations. Mass data collection and surveillance come with the question of invasion of privacy and the potential abuse of power. While data collection might be justified for the sake of national security, there must be checks and balances to ensure that the data isn't misused. The challenge is to create an ecosystem where AI can assist national security agencies without infringing upon the rights of individual citizens.

AI and Counterterrorism

Counterterrorism is one area where AI could offer significant advantages. Algorithms can scan social media, online forums, and communication channels for keywords or patterns that could indicate terrorist activity. However, this also raises concerns regarding profiling and data accuracy. If the AI is trained on biased data or is not correctly configured, it could disproportionately flag certain groups or individuals leading to unwarranted scrutiny.

Cybersecurity and AI

In the age of digital warfare, cybersecurity has become a significant concern for governments worldwide. AI can both be a weapon and a shield in this domain. Sophisticated algorithms can detect unusual patterns in data traffic, signaling potential threats. On the flip side, malicious AI can be used to hack into systems, outmaneuvering traditional security measures. Here lies another ethical dilemma—how to regulate the use of AI in cyber warfare. Should there be international laws that govern AI warfare, similar to the conventions for nuclear or biological weapons?

Ethics and Regulation

As AI becomes increasingly integrated into our national security apparatus, it will be crucial to establish frameworks for ethical use. This may include internal and external oversight, transparency in algorithmic decision-making, and public disclosure of AI use-cases in surveillance and security.

One possible solution cou d be the creation of an independent committee that reviews the use of AI in national security. This committee could consist of experts from various fields, such as technology, law, ethics, and sociology, ensuring a multi-dimensional perspective on the issues at hand.

Public Perception and Trust

Finally, how the public perceives the use of AI in matters of national security will play a significant role in its successful deployment. Transparency is key. The government must openly communicate the extent and limitations of AI usage in surveillance and security to maintain public trust.

By navigating these intricate ethical and societal issues carefully, we can harness the power of AI to make our nations more secure while respecting the privacy and freedom of its citizens.

International Cooperation and AI

In the context of national security, international cooperation is pivotal. With the increasingly interconnected world, no country exists in isolation. Therefore, the role of AI extends beyond national boundaries. Collaborative efforts, perhaps under the auspices of international organizations, could be a way to standardize the ethical and responsible use of AI in surveillance and security. Information sharing across countries can lead to a more effective global counterterrorism strategy, but it also opens up a Pandora's box of ethical concerns around data privacy across different jurisdictions.

AI technologies could allow for real-time sharing of security threats, thereby enhancing glcbal security. However, the implications of such interconnectedness need to be considered carefully. Questions surrounding data sovereignty, misuse of information, and what constitutes a 'threat' can be exceedingly complex when multiple nations are involved.

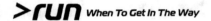

The Economic Implications

The integration of AI in national security also has economic repercussions. Developing, maintaining, and updating AI systems require significant investments. While wealthy nations might have the resources to keep up-to-date with the latest AI technologies, underfunded agencies or developing nations may fall behind, leading to a technological gap that could have serious implications for global security. Therefore, any discussions about AI in national security should also involve equitable access to technology.

Moreover, there's a risk of an AI arms race, where countries compete to develop increasingly powerful and sophisticated AI tools for national security. Such a race could not only escalate global tensions but also divert resources from other crucial areas like education, healthcare, and social welfare.

Privacy vs. Security: The Eternal Debate

The tug-of-war between individual privacy and collective security is not new, but AI adds a new dimension to this debate. How do we balance the two, and where do we draw the line? Could there be a 'Goldilocks Zone,' a just-right level of AI surveillance that maximizes security without eroding privacy?

It's crucial for democratic societies to engage in open dialogues about these issues. Perhaps referenda or public consultations could be a way to gauge public opinion on the acceptable limits of AI in national security.

AI has enormous potential to revolutionize the way nations approach security and surveillance. However, its integration into this sector is fraught with ethical, legal, and societal challenges that must be thoughtfully addressed. The conversation around these issues is just beginning, and it's essential for all stakeholders—governments, technologists, ethicists, and the general public—to engage in a transparent, informed, and nuanced dialogue.

By working together, we can create an environment where AI serves as a robust tool for national security, one that respects individual liberties and promotes international cooperation.

Ethical War or Oxymoron?

The concept of "ethical war" might seem like an oxymoron. War, by its very nature, involves violence and loss, often on a massive scale. Nonetheless, just war theory has existed for centuries, providing moral guidelines for the initiation and conduct of warfare. The incorporation of AI into military systems introduces complex variables that demand scrutiny under the lens of just war theory.

Traditionally, just war theory focuses on principles like just cause, proportionality, and necessity. These principles help ensure that wars are fought for legitimate reasons and that the use of force is measured and appropriate. AI's capacity to collect and analyze vast amounts of data could, in theory, assist military leaders in making decisions that are more aligned with the principles of just war theory.

However, this technology also poses new risks. Machine learning algorithms may inadvertently reinforce the biases of their human programmers or the data they've been trained on, leading to disproportionate or unjust attacks. Autonomous systems can malfunction, causing unintended casualties.

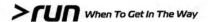

Furthermore, AI could make warfare more asymmetric, widening the gap between nations with advanced technological capabilities and those without. Imagine a scenario where a nation deploys swarms of AI-powered drones capable of identifying and eliminating targets with minimal human oversight. Such a technological advantage could lead to a rapid, perhaps decisive, victory. But what are the ethical implications? Would this be a just war, fought in a proportionate manner, or would it be an example of overpowering force exerted without adequate moral consideration?

In this chapter, we've barely scratched the surface of the issues surrounding the military use of AI. These problems are not purely academic; they have real-world implications that affect lives, international relations, and the ethical fabric of our societies. It's crucial that we continue to engage with these topics critically, bringing together perspectives from the fields of technology, ethics, law, and politics.

While AI offers unparalleled advantages in data collection and processing, its application in warfare cannot be detached from the human element—our values, ethics, and laws. If we abdicate our responsibility to guide and control these powerful tools, we risk losing sight of what makes us human in the pursuit of what makes us powerful.

As we venture deeper into this new technological landscape, it becomes clear that the decisions we make today will shape the ethical contours of tomorrow's conflicts. Let us proceed with caution, wisdom, and an unwavering commitment to justice.

The Future of International Agreements

While nations have always competed for military superiority, the addition of AI to the arsenal raises new questions about international agreements and arms control. In a world where a single line of code can potentially cause more damage than traditional weapons, how do we regulate the military use of AI?

Historically, international agreements like the Geneva Conventions have provided a framework for ethical conduct in warfare. However, these agreements were drafted in a world where AI was the stuff of science fiction. As AI becomes an increasingly integral part of military strategies, there's a growing need for new norms and agreements that specifically address the ethical and legal implications of AI in warfare.

Several nations and international organizations are beginning to recognize this need. Preliminary discussions about regulating autonomous weapons and AI-based surveillance technologies are taking place in various global forums. These conversations are fraught with complexities, as nations must weigh their security interests against ethical concerns and the potential for AI to be used in ways that are fundamentally inhumane.

Moreover, regulating AI in the military sphere also has implications for civilian sectors. Many technologies initially developed for military applications eventually find their way into civilian life. GPS and the internet are two prime examples of this phenomenon. Consequently, decisions made in the context of military AI will likely reverberate through society, affecting everything from healthcare to transportation.

Conclusion

The integration of AI into military operations is a complex and multi-faceted issue that intersects with ethics, law, and geopolitics. While AI has the potential to revolutionize warfare, making it more efficient and possibly more aligned with just war principles, it also introduces a host of ethical and legal dilemmas that we are only beginning to understand.

In this chapter, we've delved into several key aspects of this issue, from the practicalities of integrating AI into existing military systems to the ethical implications of doing so. We've also looked at the potential for international agreements to provide a framework for the ethical use of AI in warfare. The one certainty in this rapidly evolving field is that the dialogue must continue, involving not just policymakers and military leaders, but also ethicists, legal experts, and the public.

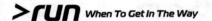

As we develop increasingly advanced AI technologies, we must also advance our ethical frameworks and legal systems to keep pace. Only by doing so can we hope to wield the immense power of AI responsibly, in a way that aligns with our most deeply held values and principles.

Chapter 10: The AI Talent War and Education

Introduction

In a world increasingly influenced by artificial intelligence, the scramble for AI talent is not limited to companies and research institutions; it has become a matter of national interest. Governments globally recognize the role that skilled human capital plays in maintaining a competitive edge in AI technology. This chapter will explore how nations are approaching the so-called "AI Talent War," focusing on the role of education, from K-12 to higher education and beyond.

The AI Skills Gap

Today, demand for AI skills far outstrips supply. According to various industry reports, millions of AI and data science roles remain unfilled globally. This skills gap is a pressing concern for businesses, but it also has national security implications. A country's ability to innovate, protect its digital assets, and remain economically competitive is intrinsically linked to the talent it can either produce or attract.

The skills gap exists at multiple levels. On the one hand, there is a shortage of highly specialized experts capable of pushing the boundaries of AI research. On the other hand, there is also a lack of professionals with the basic skills needed to implement AI solutions in various industries, including healthcare, manufacturing, and transportation.

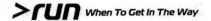

The Importance of Early Education

The foundation for AI expertise is often laid early in life. Countries like China have already begun implementing AI education in their K-12 curriculums. Basic programming is taught alongside math and science, and advanced students have the opportunity to delve into machine learning and data analysis.

But education reform is not simple. In many countries, the educational system is already strained, and teachers are not always equipped with the knowledge or resources to teach advanced topics like AI. This raises questions about educational equity: If only the best-funded schools can offer high-quality AI education, this could exacerbate existing societal inequalities.

Strategies for Higher Education

Colleges and universities are also grappling with how best to prepare students for a world where AI is ubiquitous. Traditional computer science programs have started to feel outdated, prompting curriculum reform. Interdisciplinary programs that merge computer science with fields like ethics, law, and social science are increasingly in demand. This is in line with the growing recognition that understanding AI is not just a technical endeavor but requires a broader socio-cultural understanding.

Many governments are investing heavily in their higher education systems to produce the next generation of AI researchers and professionals. For example, in the United States, the National Science Foundation has granted millions of dollars to universities to develop AI-specific courses and research projects. Similarly, the European Union has also pledged significant funding for AI research and education as part of its broader digital strategy.

Immigration and Global Talent Mobility

Skilled immigration is another facet of the AI talent war. Countries like Canada and Australia have tailored their immigration policies to attract highly skilled AI professionals. These policies often include fast-track visa programs and various incentives like tax breaks and research grants.

However, such strategies come with their own set of challenges, such as brain drain from less developed countries. Moreover, the ongoing geopolitical tensions and national security concerns have also made international collaboration more complicated. Nevertheless, the global nature of the AI talent pool makes it an imperative for nations to consider immigration as a viable strategy for securing top talent.

Public-Private Partnerships

One emerging trend in the quest to close the AI skills gap is the role of public-private partnerships. Businesses, educational institutions, and governments are collaborating more closely than ever to accelerate AI education and research. Companies are directly investing in university research, curriculum development, and even high school programs aimed at fostering AI talent. These partnerships can be incredibly effective but also raise questions about the commercialization of education and research.

Lifelong Learning and Reskilling

The fast-paced evolution of AI technology means that what is considered cutting-edge today may become obsolete tomorrow. This calls for a focus on lifelong learning and reskilling programs. Some countries are piloting innovative approaches to adult education, combining online courses, bootcamps, and on-the-job training to help workers stay relevant in an ever-changing job market.

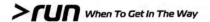

The AI talent war is a complex and multifaceted challenge that requires a strategic, long-term approach. It encompasses issues ranging from early education and higher education reform to immigration policies and public-private partnerships. As AI continues to evolve, so too must our strategies for cultivating the human talent needed to harness its potential responsibly and effectively. The stakes are high, and the outcome will undoubtedly influence not only the global economic landscape but also the ethical and societal implications of AI's broader role in our lives.

AI Ethics Education: The New Frontier

As AI systems become increasingly complex and integrated into various aspects of life, the need for ethical considerations in the development and deployment of these technologies is paramount. Thus, AI ethics education is emerging as a new educational frontier that transcends technical skills. This section aims to delve into the initiatives, programs, and curriculum designs aimed at embedding ethics into AI education.

A unique challenge here is to balance technical depth with ethical nuance. Programs such as MIT's Ethics of AI course or Stanford's Ethical and Social Issues in Natural Language Processing are prime examples. These courses aim to equip students not only with the skills to build AI models but also the ability to evaluate and mitigate their societal impacts.

The Role of Government in AI Education

Governments worldwide are starting to recognize the importance of funding and supporting AI education at all levels. This involves not only financial aid but also formulating strategic policies that aim to position a country as a global AI leader.

Initiatives range from K-12 education grants to substantial funding for university research. Policy frameworks are also being created to guide ethical considerations in AI, inform public opinion, and provide a stable environment for AI investments. However, with these opportunities come the challenge of bureaucracy, the need for agility in decision-making, and alignment with fast-paced technological developments.

Global Collaboration: A Path Forward

Given the global nature of the challenges posed by AI, international collaboration becomes essential. Programs like the AI for Good Summit by the United Nations aim to bring together experts, policymakers, and educators to brainstorm solutions that can be adopted globally. Here, the key is to foster an environment that transcends geopolitical differences and focuses on the common goal of ethical and equitable AI development.

Collaboration also brings the advantage of shared resources. This includes open-source AI educational materials, multi-country research projects, and the formation of international standards and best practices. Yet, this international approach faces hurdles in the form of political climates, differing educational standards, and conflicting national interests.

Private Sector Involvement: A Double-Edged Sword

The private sector's role in AI education brings both opportunities and challenges. Companies often provide much-needed financial resources and expertise, but their involvement also poses questions about the influence they might have on educational content and research direction. For instance, is it ethical for a tech company to sponsor a university course that may directly benefit its proprietary technologies?

An ideal partnership would involve transparent agreements that prioritize educational outcomes over business interests. Examples of this can be seen in IBM's P-TECH schools or Google's AI for Social Good initiative, where the focus is on broader societal benefits rather than immediate commercial gains.

The quest for AI talent is a multi-dimensional challenge requiring a concerted effort from all stakeholders involved. From early education to workforce reskilling, from national policies to global collaborations, the pathways are varied but interconnected. As we move forward, it becomes crucial to address these aspects comprehensively to ensure not just the development of AI technologies, but also their ethical and equitable application for the benefit of society at large.

The Changing Landscape of AI Jobs

As AI technologies continue to evolve, the job market is undergoing a significant transformation. Traditional roles in data science and machine learning are giving way to more specialized positions that require an in-depth understanding of specific AI technologies or domains. For example, AI ethics officers and AI auditors are emerging as crucial roles in organizations, ensuring the responsible use of AI. These new roles underscore the need for interdisciplinary skills, blending technical expertise with ethical and legal know-how.

The AI field has been criticized for its lack of gender diversity, with reports indicating that women make up less than 20% of the workforce in some areas of AI research and development. This is not just a social issue; it's also a matter of business efficacy and fairness. A homogenous group of developers can lead to biased algorithms, which can further exacerbate social inequalities. Numerous organizations and initiatives are working to bridge this gap by promoting STEM education for girls and creating mentorship programs for women in AI.

Soft skills like communicat on, critical thinking, and empathy are becoming increasingly important in the AI field. Whether it's explaining complex algorithms to non-technical stakeholders or understanding the societal implications of a particular AI application, these skills are crucial for the ethical and responsible development and deployment of AI technologies. Educational programs need to incorporate soft skills training as a mandatory part of the curriculum to prepare students for the multi-disciplinary nature of future AI work.

Accessibility and Inclusivity in AI Education

As AI continues to influence every sector of society, ensuring that AI education is accessible to all becomes a significant concern. Online courses and MOOCs are making AI education more accessible, but they are not a complete solut on. The digital divide, especially in developing countries, is a barrier that still needs to be overcome. Efforts must be made to include marginalized communities in AI education to ensure a diverse workforce that can address a wide array of challenges.

In a field that is changing as rapidly as AI, the concept of lifelong learning becomes incredibly important. Professionals need to be adaptable and willing to update their skills continuously. In this context, educational systems must evolve to provide opportunities for ongoing education in AI, such as short-term courses, workshops, and online resources. Lifelong learning is not just a necessity but a survival skill in the rapidly evolving landscape of AI.

While it's critical to have separate courses focusing on the ethics of AI, integrating ethical considerations into technical courses can provide a more holistic education. Students should be taught to think critically about the ethical implications of their work at every stage of their educational journey. This dual focus will help students become not just skilled technicians but responsible citizens who can use AI for the greater good.

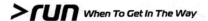

AI Literacy for the General Public

As AI becomes an integral part of daily life, a basic understanding of AI is becoming as essential as reading and writing. Therefore, AI literacy programs aimed at the general public are crucial. These programs should focus on helping people understand how AI impacts their lives and how they can make informed decisions about using AI technologies.

AI is not just a field of computer science; it intersects with various other disciplines, including psychology, neuroscience, ethics, and law. Therefore, an interdisciplinary approach is critical for a well-rounded AI education. Institutions are increasingly offering joint degrees or special programs that combine AI with other fields, giving students a broader perspective and a more versatile skillset.

The Commercial Aspects of AI Education

In today's world, AI isn't just an academic subject; it has enormous commercial implications as well. As such, a thorough AI education should also cover the business aspects of AI technologies. This includes everything from how startups can leverage AI to gain a competitive edge, to how large corporations can integrate AI into their existing workflows for increased efficiency and better decision-making. Future courses could focus on case studies that offer real-world examples of AI in the business realm, providing students with a well-rounded view of the field.

Regulatory Implications and Compliance

As AI technologies get more sophisticated, they increasingly intersect with regulatory frameworks. From data protection laws like the GDPR to specific guidelines around the use of AI in healthcare or autonomous driving, understanding the regulatory landscape is crucial for anyone involved in AI. Therefore, a comprehensive AI education must include topics on regulatory compliance, possibly offering certifications that attest to an individual's understanding of these matters.

AI in Healthcare Education

One sector that is particularly impacted by AI is healthcare. From diagnostics to treatment plans, AI technologies are gradually becoming a significant part of the medical field. Educational programs should include specialized tracks for healthcare professionals, covering topics like the role of AI in medical imaging, disease identification, and personalized medicine. Such courses can be invaluable in ensuring the ethical and efficient application of AI in healthcare.

AI in the Creative Industries

Another interesting facet of AI is its application in creative fields like art, music, and writing. While these are not traditionally areas where one would expect to find algorithms at work, AI technologies like neural networks have begun to create art and compose music. Courses that explore these applications can provide a completely different perspective on what AI can achieve, dispelling the notion that it is merely a tool for number crunching.

The Importance of Open-Source in AI Education

The open-source movement has been pivotal in the development of AI technologies. Many of the most critical advancements in AI have come from open-source projects, and it's crucial for students to understand the importance of this community-driven model. Not only does it promote collaboration and speed up innovation, but it also offers a platform for students to gain practical experience. Working on open-source projects could be a recommended or even required component of AI education programs.

AI education is a vast and rapidly evolving field that intersects with numerous other disciplines and sectors. Its future is bound to be as dynamic as the technologies it aims to teach. As educators, policymakers, and professionals, we must be willing to adapt and grow along with it, ensuring that future generations are well-equipped to navigate a world where AI is increasingly omnipresent.

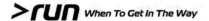

AI Ethics and Societal Implications

In the 21st century, it's not enough to understand AI from a technical perspective alone. As the technology integrates more deeply into our everyday lives, its ethical and societal implications become more urgent to address. AI systems can perpetuate bias, infringe upon privacy, and even present existential risks if not carefully managed. This makes the inclusion of ethics in any AI educational program not just an optional add-on, but a necessity.

Courses on AI ethics should dissect real-world scenarios where AI algorithms have resulted in unintended negative consequences, such as racial or gender bias in hiring algorithms or law enforcement applications. Ethical considerations should be a thread running through all AI courses, allowing students to understand the full scope and impact of the technologies they may one day create or manage. Here, philosophy can meet technology, offering essential tools for ethical decision-making and critical thinking.

The Need for Interdisciplinary Education

The multifaceted nature of AI demands an interdisciplinary approach to education. While strong technical skills in mathematics, data science, and programming are fundamental, a well-rounded AI education should also include elements of psychology, philosophy, ethics, and even art and humanities. This interdisciplinary model would better prepare students for the complexities of real-world AI applications, which often span multiple sectors and require diverse skill sets to understand fully.

Moreover, it's essential for students to learn how to collaborate across disciplines. Engineers should understand the ethical implications of their work, just as ethicists should understand the fundamental technologies that they critique. These interdisciplinary programs would aim to produce a new generation of AI professionals who are as comfortable discussing Kantian ethics as they are fine-tuning a neural network.

116

The Role of Simulations and Practical Experience

While theoretical knowledge forms the backbone of any educational program, AI education is incomplete without hands-on experience. Virtual labs, simulations, and real-world projects should be integral parts of the curriculum. Not only do these practical exercises provide students with valuable experience, but they also help to demystify AI technologies, making them more approachable and less abstract. For example, by building a simple chatbot or creating a basic image recognition model, students can gain a tangible understanding of the underlying algorithms and processes, making the theory more accessible.

International Perspectives in AI Education

In an increasingly interconnected world, AI technologies do not respect national borders. Therefore, AI education should also have a global perspective, incorporating case studies, ethical considerations, and regulations from around the world. Students should learn about how AI technologies are applied and governed in different cultural and regulatory environments, such as the European Union, China, or African nations. Understanding these international nuances can prepare students for a global job market and offer a more rounded view of AI's worldwide impact.

Conclusion

The future of AI education is not set in stone; it will evolve along with the technology itself. As AI continues to change the world in both subtle and profound ways, our approach to educating the next generation of AI experts must adapt. The considerations outlined in this chapter aim to serve as a roadmap for developing a more comprehensive, ethical, and interdisciplinary AI education. By taking into account the rapid advancements in the field, the complex ethical landscape, and the need for a multifaceted educational approach, we can better prepare students for the inevitable challenges and opportunities that AI will bring.

Chapter 11: Ethical and Societal Implications of AI in Healthcare

Transparency and Accountability

In the vast ecosystem of healthcare, the introduction of Artificial Intelligence (AI) brings about a cascade of complexities around transparency and accountability. This is not just a computational problem to be solved; it's a multi-layered challenge that has both technical and human elements.

Traditionally, medical decisions have been made by human professionals, making it relatively straightforward to trace back the rationale behind each decision. In contrast, AI algorithms often operate as "black boxes," with their decision-making processes being largely opaque. In an industry as critical as healthcare, this lack of transparency can be a significant issue, as clinicians and patients alike need to understand how and why a particular decision was made.

It's essential to separate transparency into its constituent parts for better understanding. First, there's the transparency of the data—where it comes from, how it's cleaned and curated, and who has access to it. Many healthcare AI applications rely on large datasets, often sourced from multiple locations, each with their privacy policies and patient demographics. This creates a situation where not all stakeholders may have the same level of visibility into the data, raising questions about data accuracy and representativeness.

Next, there's the algorithmic transparency, which requires the algorithm to be interpretable by humans. Companies developing healthcare AI solutions are often hesitant to make their algorithms fully transparent due to proprietary concerns. This results in a significant tension between corporate interests and societal needs for transparency. The push for more open standards and interpretability features in AI models is gaining traction but is yet to become the industry norm.

Finally, there's the transparency in decision-making and accountability. In the traditional healthcare setting, it's relatively clear who is accountable for medical decisions: the healthcare provider. However, the introduction of AI complicates this, as the software developers and the healthcare providers share the responsibility. It's yet unclear how legal systems will adapt to this new reality, and various scholars and industry experts propose frameworks to make the lines of accountability more apparent.

These three facets of transparency contribute to a complex interplay of technical and ethical challenges that have far-reaching implications for all stakeholders involved. Developing universally accepted standards for transparency and accountability could take years, if not decades, but the conversation needs to start now. If not, we risk creating a healthcare ecosystem where critical decisions affecting human lives are made behind closed doors, with little to no oversight.

Bias and Fairness

As we venture further into the implementation of AI in healthcare, the issue of bias becomes increasingly salient. Bias can manifest in many forms—data bias, algorithmic bias, and systemic bias, to name a few—and has far-reaching implications for patient outcomes and healthcare disparities.

Let's first examine data bias. AI algorithms are only as good as the data they are trained on. If the training data is not representative of the population it serves, the algorithm can produce biased results. For instance, an AI model trained primarily on Caucasian male data will be less accurate when used for females or other ethnic groups.

However, data bias is only the tip of the iceberg. Even if the data is well-balanced, algorithmic biases can still occur. Algorithmic bias refers to situations where the algorithm itself perpetuates a form of bias, regardless of the fairness of the data it's trained on. Machine learning models are designed to identify patterns in data; if those patterns include societal biases, the model will learn and replicate those biases.

Bias and fairness cannot be fully understood without also discussing systemic bias. In many healthcare systems globally, there are existing disparities in healthcare accessibility, affordability, and quality. When AI systems are implemented in such environments, there's a risk of exacerbating these disparities. For example, an AI system trained in a high-income country may not perform well in a low-income setting, further widening the gap between the quality of healthcare services available to different socio-economic groups.

Addressing bias in healthcare AI is not just a data science problem; it's an issue that needs multi-disciplinary expertise, including insights from social science, ethics, and law. Ongoing efforts to improve data representativeness and algorithmic fairness are crucial steps towards a more equitable healthcare system.

Scalability and Integration

Adopting AI in healthcare is not a plug-and-play operation; it requires a substantial transformation of existing systems—both technical and human. This makes scalability and integration some of the most challenging aspects of AI adoption in healthcare.

One of the primary issues is data compatibility. Healthcare data is often stored in various formats across different systems. A large hospital might have one system for patient records, another for billing, and yet another for radiology images. Before any AI system can be effectively implemented, these disparate data sources must be harmonized, a task easier said than done.

Apart from data compatibility, there's the challenge of system compatibility. Existing healthcare infrastructures often utilize outdated software or hardware that may not be compatible with state-of-the-art AI applications. The financial cost of upgrading these systems can be a significant barrier for many healthcare providers, particularly those in lower-income settings.

Then there's the human element. Healthcare professionals need to be trained not only to use the new AI-powered systems but also to trust them. This entails a considerable investment in education and change management strategies, as many healthcare professionals are accustomed to traditional methods and may be resistant to relying on an algorithm for medical decision-making.

All these issues contribute to the complexity of scaling and integrating AI into existing healthcare ecosystems. Despite these challenges, the potential benefits of AI-powered healthcare solutions make the pursuit worthwhile. Efforts are underway to create more standardized, interoperable systems that can better accommodate AI applications, but this is a long-term effort that will require cooperation across sectors.

Data Privacy and Security

One of the most critical concerns when implementing AI in healthcare is the issue of data privacy and security. Health data is sensitive and often subject to stringent legal regulations. AI's reliance on big data exacerbates this concern. The more data an AI system has, the better it can potentially perform, but this also increases the risk of data breaches or misuse.

Several high-profile cases have exposed the vulnerabilities in healthcare data systems. Not only do such breaches compromise the privacy of individuals, but they also pose serious ethical questions about who owns this data and how it should be used. Patients have a right to know where their data is stored, who has access to it, and for what purposes it is being used.

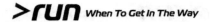

Emerging technologies like blockchain promise better data security and ownership solutions but are far from being universally implemented. The existing systems are often not adequately equipped to protect against the sophisticated hacking techniques used today. As AI systems continue to integrate with healthcare databases, there will be a growing need for sophisticated cybersecurity measures, along with consistent updates and monitoring to protect against emerging threats.

Even if the technical challenges of data security are met, the ethical dilemmas remain. Should insurance companies have access to AI-derived data that could predict a patient's future health risks? What kind of consent should be obtained from patients, and how should they be informed about the ways their data could be used—or misused? As AI becomes more pervasive in healthcare, society must grapple with these ethical implications to ensure that technological advancements don't come at the cost of individual rights or social inequalities.

Global Health and AI

AI has the potential to revolutionize not only healthcare in developed countries but also to significantly impact global health. Many developing countries face severe healthcare challenges, including limited access to medical facilities, scarcity of trained healthcare professionals, and prevalence of infectious diseases. AI could be a game-changer in these settings by extending healthcare capabilities where they are most needed.

Telemedicine, powered by AI, can enable healthcare professionals to diagnose and treat patients in remote areas. Algorithms can analyze medical images or data remotely, providing vital support to understaffed local medical facilities. In addition, AI can also assist in tracking and predicting the spread of infectious diseases, helping to allocate resources more effectively during outbreaks.

However, the deployment of AI in these settings brings its own set of challenges. There's the risk of creating a "tech divide," where only those with access to AI-powered healthcare can benefit from its advantages. Additionally, solutions developed in and for high-income countries may not be directly transferable to lower-income settings, necessitating local adaptation and validation of AI algorithms.

In the push to globalize AI in healthcare, it's crucial to remember that ethical and societal implications are not universal but contextual. What is considered ethical or acceptable in one culture may not be so in another, and AI systems must be sensitive to these nuances. This requires a multi-disciplinary, multi-stakeholder approach, where technologists collaborate with ethicists, healthcare providers, and community representatives to tailor AI solutions to specific societal contexts.

Transparency and Accountability in AI Healthcare Applications

Transparency and accountability in healthcare AI systems are not just ethical imperatives but are often legally required. Patients have a right to know the basis on which a healthcare decision about them was made, particularly when AI is involved in the decision-making process. There's a burgeoning debate among ethicists, healthcare providers, and technologists on how to make the complex algorithms more interpretable to non-experts. Various methods are being proposed and tested to make black-box algorithms more transparent, ranging from simplified summary statistics to complex graphical interfaces that visualize the algorithm's decision-making process.

Further complicating the matter is the concept of accountability. If an AI system makes a mistake, who is responsible? Is it the healthcare provider using the tool, the organization implementing it, or the developers who designed the algorithm? These questions have significant implications for medical malpractice laws, which have not yet evolved to address the complexities introduced by AI.

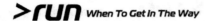

The American Medical Association and the World Health Organization are among the entities that have started to draft guidelines regarding the ethical use of AI in healthcare, including aspects of transparency and accountability. However, these guidelines are far from being universally accepted or implemented. Until that happens, the ambiguity surrounding these issues will remain a significant challenge in the widespread adoption of AI in healthcare.

AI's Impact on Healthcare Jobs

Another angle that needs thorough examination is the impact of AI on healthcare employment. The fear of job loss due to automation isn't new, but in the context of healthcare, it takes on a different dimension. Healthcare is a sector that employs millions of people worldwide, and the integration of AI could potentially disrupt this labor market. While some jobs may become obsolete, others could undergo significant transformation, requiring healthcare professionals to acquire new skill sets to work alongside AI systems.

For example, diagnostic radiologists, who are already using AI to assist in identifying abnormalities in X-rays and MRIs, may find their roles evolving. They might transition into more consultative roles, guiding therapeutic decisions rather than primarily focusing on diagnosis. However, the shift won't happen overnight and will require retraining and educational programs to help healthcare workers adapt to the new landscape.

Labor unions, educational institutions, and healthcare organizations are starting to recognize the need for new training programs. Pilot programs in various parts of the world are aiming to retrain healthcare workers, but these are still in the nascent stages. Until a structured pathway is established for healthcare professionals to adapt to an AI-integrated environment, the labor market will remain in a state of flux, causing anxiety and uncertainty among healthcare workers.

Ethical Dilemmas Surrounding Data Privacy

Another significant issue in the realm of AI in healthcare is data privacy. The scale at which data are collected and analyzed poses an inherent risk to patient confidentiality. Data breaches, unauthorized access, and misuse of data are realistic threats that healthcare providers and AI developers must address. Comprehensive cybersecurity measures are vital, but even with state-of-the-art security protocols, the risk is never entirely eliminated.

In the United States, the Health Insurance Portability and Accountability Act (HIPAA) provides a legal framework to protect patient data. However, these regulations were not designed with the complexities of AI and big data in mind. The legislation struggles to address the unique challenges posed by machine learning algorithms, which often require access to large amounts of data, sometimes from multiple institutions, for training and validation. The European Union's General Data Protection Regulation (GDPR) also offers some guidance, but it too falls short in the context of healthcare AI.

Efforts are underway to amend existing laws and formulate new ones that adequately address data privacy concerns in healthcare AI. Still, legislative processes are often slow and fraught with political complexities. Lobbying by technology companies and other vested interests also influences these processes, further complicating the situation. The lack of clear, robust legislation means that healthcare providers and AI developers are often left to navigate a murky legal landscape, complicating efforts to deploy AI solutions in a way that is both effective and ethical.

The Economic Implications of AI in Healthcare

The economic aspects of implementing AI in healthcare are multi-faceted and worth serious consideration. On the one hand, AI has the potential to bring down costs by automating routine tasks, improving diagnostic accuracy, and optimizing resource allocation. On the other hand, the initial investment in AI technology can be prohibitively expensive for smaller healthcare providers, widening the gap between large healthcare systems and smaller practices.

Moreover, there's the question of whether the cost savings realized by AI will translate to lower healthcare costs for patients. In a profit-driven healthcare system, there's no guarantee that providers will pass on these savings to consumers. In systems where healthcare is publicly funded, budgetary considerations could lead to AI being implemented in a way that prioritizes cost-saving over other ethical considerations, such as patient autonomy or data privacy.

Studies have shown that the potential for cost-saving in healthcare through AI is enormous. According to a report by the advisory firm Accenture, AI applications in healthcare could create up to $150 billion in annual savings for the United States healthcare economy by 2026. However, these figures are speculative and based on the assumption that the technology will be implemented widely and efficiently, which is far from certain given the various challenges discussed earlier in this chapter.

Liability and Accountability in AI-Driven Healthcare

As healthcare increasingly relies on AI, questions about liability and accountability become more complex. Traditional models for determining medical liability usually focus on human error. But what happens when an AI system is responsible for a medical mistake? The legal frameworks for addressing such issues are still underdeveloped, leading to a confusing landscape that can deter healthcare providers from adopting new technologies.

Manufacturers, software developers, healthcare providers, and even patients themselves could all conceivably bear some responsibility when things go wrong. Some experts propose that AI systems should have a 'black box' recording mechanism to help trace decision-making processes in the event of an adverse outcome. However, the opaqueness of certain machine learning algorithms can make it difficult to ascertain the cause of a particular decision, complicating liability issues.

Ethical considerations also play into this conversation. Should a machine be allowed to make life-and-death decisions? If so, what kind of oversight should exist? The implementation of ethical guidelines, perhaps modeled on existing frameworks for human medical ethics, is one avenue being explored. However, the lack of a standardized approach across different jurisdictions and healthcare systems makes universal adoption difficult.

AI and the Future of the Medical Workforce

AI's role in automating tasks extends to the medical workforce and introduces new concerns about job displacement. While AI can handle data analysis and even some diagnostic tasks, the 'human touch' in healthcare remains irreplaceable for now. Emotional intelligence, the ability to comfort and reassure patients, and ethical decision-making are all aspects of healthcare that are uniquely human.

However, as AI systems become more advanced, it's conceivable that many tasks currently performed by healthcare professionals could be automated. A 2019 study by McKinsey estimated that up to 30% of the tasks performed by nurses and up to 20% of those performed by doctors could potentially be automated. While automation could alleviate workforce shortages in some areas, it also raises concerns about job losses and the de-skilling of the medical profession.

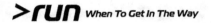

Training programs for healthcare professionals may need to evolve to include a focus on skills that are complementary to AI, such as data interpretation, ethics, and patient communication. These skills will not only enhance the capabilities of healthcare professionals but also ensure that they remain an indispensable part of the healthcare ecosystem.

Solving Common Employee Issues through Categorization

As an AI leader, you'll frequently encounter challenges that are common to almost any leadership position, but they come with an added layer of complexity due to the nature of AI projects. Addressing common employee issues effectively is crucial for maintaining high morale and productivity within your team.

1. **Conflict Resolution**: In a field as interdisciplinary and rapidly evolving as AI, conflicts are almost inevitable. A data scientist may not understand the challenges that an engineer is facing in deploying a model, or a business stakeholder may have unrealistic expectations about what a certain algorithm can achieve. Understanding the source of conflicts and creating a culture of open dialogue can solve many issues before they escalate.

2. **Skill Development:** AI is a field that continuously evolves. Today's cutting-edge algorithms might become obsolete in a year. Ensuring that your team is continually learning and growing professionally is key to staying relevant.

3. **Burnout:** Due to the often intense and high-stakes nature of AI projects, burnout is a common issue. Identifying early signs and implementing preventative measures can make a significant difference.

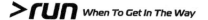

4. **Retention:** In a highly competitive market for AI talent, retaining your skilled employees is more critical than ever. Competitive salaries, professional growth opportunities, and work-life balance all play a role.

5. **Cultural Fit:** With diverse teams often spread across different geographies and time zones, creating a cohesive company culture can be challenging. Organizational strategies must adapt to fit these unique circumstances, taking into consideration the different cultural backgrounds and values of team members.

Solving these common challenges often requires a nuanced understanding of both the technical and human factors involved. Tailoring your leadership style to effectively manage and guide your team is a skill that comes with experience but can be significantly aided by the strategic application of AI tools. Whether it's using AI to predict potential conflicts or to tailor employee development programs, the power of AI can be harnessed to solve traditional managerial challenges in novel ways.

Ethical Considerations

Leading an AI team also means navigating the murky waters of ethics in AI. Ethical concerns are increasingly becoming a focal point in the world of AI, and rightfully so. As a leader, it's your responsibility to ensure that your team adheres to ethical standards when developing and deploying AI solutions. Whether it's issues of data privacy, algorithmic bias, or the social implications of AI, a well-rounded leader must have a strong ethical compass and the ability to navigate these complex issues.

1. **Data Privacy:** In the age of big data, concerns about data privacy are at an all-time high. As a leader, it's your responsibility to ensure that your team is handling data ethically and legally.

2. **Algorithmic Bias:** Machine learning models can inherit the biases present in their training data or their designers. Leaders must be vigilant in monitoring for such biases and committed to addressing them when they arise.

3. **Social Implications:** AI has the potential to significantly impact society, for better or worse. Thoughtful leadership in AI extends beyond the lab or boardroom and considers the broader societal implications of the technologies being developed.

4. **Regulatory Compliance:** AI is increasingly becoming subject to various forms of regulation. Staying compliant while innovating can be a delicate balancing act requiring sound leadership skills.

Ethical leadership in AI goes beyond mere compliance with laws and regulations. It also involves a deep understanding of the potential impact of your work, a commitment to doing what is right, and the courage to take a stand when faced with ethical dilemmas.

In Conclusion

In conclusion, leadership in the realm of AI comes with its unique set of challenges and opportunities that extend far beyond the traditional norms of management. As a leader steering an AI-focused team, your responsibilities are manifold, encompassing not just technical and project management, but also ethical stewardship, employee development, and conflict resolution. Each of these elements plays a critical role in building a successful, harmonious, and ethically sound AI team. This chapter has provided you with comprehensive insights and actionable strategies to navigate the intricacies of AI leadership successfully.

The future of AI is incredibly promising but equally fraught with complexity and ethical concerns. As you lead your team through this ever-evolving landscape, your leadership will be the beacon that guides them not just towards technological advancements but also ethical integrity. As we have emphasized, balancing these elements is no small feat, but with the right approach and tools at your disposal, you'll be well-equipped to lead your team to new heights, ensuring that your AI projects are not only successful but also beneficial for society at large.

Your leadership journey in the world of AI is an ongoing process of learning, adapting, and growing. So as you turn the page, keep an open mind and a committed spirit, for every challenge you face is an opportunity for you and your team to evolve and excel.

In the chapters to come, we will delve deeper into more specific aspects of AI leadership, including the importance of continuous learning and how to manage an AI project from inception to deployment effectively. So, stay tuned as we continue to equip you with the knowledge and skills you need to be an exemplary AI leader.

Chapter 12: Continuous Learning: A Core Competency in AI Leadership

Introduction

In the fast-paced world of artificial intelligence, the landscape is continually evolving. New algorithms are developed, computing power increases, and ethical considerations become more complex. As a leader in the AI sector, one of your most crucial roles is to ensure that both you and your team are continuously learning and adapting to these changes. This chapter will explore why continuous learning is a core competency in AI leadership, how to cultivate a culture of continuous learning within your organization, and the tools and resources available to support this endeavor.

The Imperative for Continuous Learning in AI

In many fields, once you've reached a position of leadership, the focus often shifts from individual skills development to broader managerial tasks such as team-building, strategy, and oversight. While these aspects are undeniably essential in AI as well, the rapidly evolving nature of the technology makes continuous learning non-negotiable. Whether it's keeping abreast of the latest algorithms, understanding changes in data privacy laws, or learning about new applications of AI in different sectors, a commitment to ongoing education is vital.

This constant learning isn't just for your benefit. A leader's commitment to education signals to the team the importance of staying updated, ultimately fostering a culture where everyone is motivated to expand their skill set and knowledge base. This collective commitment to learning not only helps maintain a competitive edge but also significantly aids in employee retention.

Cultivating a Culture of Continuous Learning

1. **Lead by Example:** The first step in creating a learning culture is to lead by example. Regularly invest time in your professional development and be open about it. Share what you're learning with your team and how it could benefit ongoing or future projects.

2. **Provide Opportunities:** Make educational resources readily available. This could range from offering in-house training sessions, reimbursing courses, or simply providing a library of relevant reading material.

3. **Encourage Knowledge Sharing:** Create platforms or forums where team members can share what they've learned. This could be a monthly meeting, a newsletter, or an internal blog.

4. **Recognize and Reward:** Acknowledge those who take the initiative to learn and apply new skills. This recognition can be financial, but often a public acknowledgment can be just as impactful.

Tools and Resources for Continuous Learning

In today's digital age, the resources for learning are abundant. Here are some avenues you can explore:

1. **Online Courses:** Websites like Coursera, Udacity, and edX offer a multitude of courses ranging from beginner to expert levels in almost every field related to AI.

2. **Webinars and Conferences:** These are excellent platforms for not just learning but also networking.

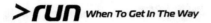
3. **Books and Journals:** With AI being a hot topic, many leading researchers and experts in the field have authored books that can provide deep insights into specialized topics.

4. **Learning Communities**: Online forums such as Reddit's Machine Learning board, or specialized AI communities can be valuable resources for problem-solving and staying updated on the latest trends.

Measuring the Impact of Continuous Learning

Implementing a culture of continuous learning is not without its challenges. One of the key issues you'll face is how to measure its impact. Start by setting clear learning objectives that align with your organizational goals. Use key performance indicators (KPIs) to measure these objectives at regular intervals.

Some commonly used KPIs include:

1. **Employee Engagement Scores:** Higher engagement often correlates with a successful learning culture.

2. **Skills Gap Analysis:** Regularly assess the skills within your team and identify where gaps have been closed or reduced.

3. **Project Outcomes:** Look for a positive correlation between the application of new knowledge and the success of projects.

By paying attention to these metrics, you can fine-tune your approach to continuous learning, ensuring that it yields tangible benefits for both the individuals in your team and the organization.

The Historical Context of Media in Politics

The use of media in politics is not a new phenomenon; it dates back to the founding fathers, who utilized newspapers and pamphlets to disseminate their messages. However, the face of political media has undergone significant changes over the years. For instance, radio and television became potent tools in the 20th century, reshaping the landscape entirely. The advent of the internet in the late 20th century and social media platforms in the 21st century has dramatically transformed how politicians engage with the electorate. This continuous evolution has consequences, both beneficial and detrimental, which we must understand to navigate the current digital political landscape.

The Affordability and Reach of Social Media

Perhaps the most prominent advantage of social media is its cost-effectiveness. Traditional media channels like TV and newspapers can be prohibitively expensive, particularly for grassroots campaigns or candidates lacking substantial financial backing. Social media, on the other hand, offers a much more affordable platform for politicians to connect with voters. Even better, the reach of social media transcends geographical limitations, allowing candidates to connect with a global audience if they wish. The 2016 U.S. Presidential campaign, for instance, saw significant international interest and involvement on social media platforms like Twitter and Facebook.

The Power of Viral Messages

Social media is unique in its ability to make messages go viral. A well-crafted tweet or a compelling Facebook post can spread like wildfire, gaining exponential exposure at no additional cost. While this virality can work to disseminate positive messages, it can also propagate misinformation, rumors, and slander. The 2020 U.S. Presidential election saw multiple instances of viral fake news stories, some of which were believed by a considerable section of the electorate, affecting perceptions and potentially voter behavior.

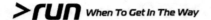

The Risks of Misinformation and Polarization

However, the use of social media in politics is not without its downsides. The same platforms that enable politicians to communicate directly with voters also serve as breeding grounds for misinformation. The spread of fake news can significantly damage a candidate's reputation and misinform the public. Furthermore, the algorithms that power these platforms often create "echo chambers" that only expose users to viewpoints similar to their own, exacerbating polarization.

Regulatory Concerns and the Way Forward

The rising importance of social media in politics has prompted calls for more stringent regulations. The issue of political advertising, data privacy, and combating misinformation are all topics of ongoing debate. Several countries are taking steps to address these concerns through legislation but finding the right balance between free speech and regulation is a complex task.

Political Campaign Strategies in the Social Media Age

In the digital age, the landscape of political campaigning has transformed dramatically. The essence of a political campaign strategy in the social media era is multi-faceted. It is not just about having a presence on social media platforms, but also about how effectively that presence is managed and utilized.

Social media has emerged as a highly efficient tool for micro-targeting. Campaigners can now identify specific groups of people and tailor messages that are more likely to resonate with them. This is facilitated by complex algorithms that process enormous amounts of data to predict user preferences and behavior. For instance, if a political campaign targets environmental sustainability, analytics can help identify social media users who have shown an interest in this subject, down to specific issues like clean energy or wildlife conservation.

Additionally, social media provides real-time feedback, something traditional campaign tools couldn't offer. This feedback comes in various forms – likes, shares, comments, and the subtle yet powerful 'sentiment analysis' provided by advanced analytics tools. Therefore, not only can campaigns disseminate information at a fraction of the cost of traditional media, but they can also gauge its immediate impact and adjust strategies accordingly.

The Ethical Dilemmas in Digital Campaigning

As we delve deeper into digital campaigning, ethical considerations become more significant and complicated. The first ethical challenge is the source of funding for these highly sophisticated digital operations. The rise of 'dark money' and the involvement of super PACs in political campaigns raise questions about transparency and the undue influence of wealthy donors.

Moreover, the scale and complexity of data analytics and AI have introduced novel ethical concerns. Machine learning algorithms, built to predict and influence voter behavior, can sometimes engage in 'racial profiling,' promoting or suppressing information based on demographics, which is an ethically dubious practice.

Issues of misinformation and fake news have become major concerns in the ethical domain of digital campaigning. Social media platforms are still grappling with controlling the spread of false information. The stakes are even higher during a political campaign, where misinformation can have direct consequences on the outcome of elections.

The Future of Political Campaigning in the Social Media Landscape

The coming years are expected to witness even more integration of sophisticated technologies in political campaigns. Virtual Reality (VR) and Augmented Reality (AR) technologies are being explored as tools for voter engagement. Imagine a future where you can participate in a virtual political rally, where the candidate appears in your living room through a VR headset.

Blockchain technology is another frontier. It promises to make campaign funding more transparent, allowing for real-time public audits of campaign donations. The next decade may witness a shift from big data to 'smart data,' characterized by more effective and ethical use of data analytics.

The use of AI will expand to create more sophisticated models of voter behavior, capable of processing emotional cues, not just factual information. This will enable campaigns to tap into the deeper, emotional layers of voter psychology, which often play an underrated role in decision-making.

Regulations Governing Digital Campaigns

In light of all the ethical concerns and the disruptive potential of technology, it's only natural that governments around the world are pushing for stronger regulations. In the United States, the Federal Election Commission (FEC) has guidelines for political advertising online, although critics argue that these are not stringent enough given the pace at which technology is evolving.

The European Union has also been proactive in implementing laws like the General Data Protection Regulation (GDPR), which places restrictions on the kind of data that can be collected and how it's used. Additionally, GDPR requires explicit consent from individuals for their data to be processed, a step that inherently places a check on micro-targeting practices.

138

However, enforcing these regulations remains a significant challenge. Many political organizations employ third-party vendors to manage their social media campaigns, making the lines of accountability blurred. This complexity is further amplified by the global nature of digital platforms, making jurisdiction a major issue.

The Role of Traditional Media

Despite the digital turn, traditional media like television, radio, and newspapers continue to have a significant impact, especially among older demographics who may not be as tech-savvy. For example, televised debates remain a cornerstone of any campaign, reaching millions of viewers.

It would be a strategic mistake for campaign managers to disregard traditional media entirely. Instead, a hybrid approach often yields the best results, where digital and traditional campaign methods are integrated to provide a comprehensive reach. For instance, social media can be used to build hype around an upcoming television interview or to provide follow-up content post-broadcast.

The Need for an Integrated Approach

Campaign managers of the future will likely require expertise in both digital and traditional forms of campaigning. The key lies in crafting a coherent message across all platforms. Inconsistencies in the campaign's message can be fatal, especially in an age where information can be disseminated widely within seconds.

An integrated approach also means constant communication and collaboration between the digital and traditional media teams within a campaign. This is particularly crucial during crises or controversies, where a coordinated response across platforms can help control the narrative and minimize damage.

The social media landscape is intricately woven into the fabric of modern political campaigning. With advancements in technology, the methodologies are continuously evolving, requiring campaign managers to adapt and innovate. Ethical and regulatory considerations further complicate the landscape, raising questions that societies must address to maintain the integrity of electoral processes.

Despite the challenges, the fusion of traditional and digital means offers unprecedented opportunities for more engaging, effective, and possibly even more democratic political campaigning, provided it is executed thoughtfully and responsibly.

Conclusion

Chapter 12 has dived deep into the multifaceted realm of modern political campaigning. As we've discussed, the landscape has evolved substantially with the advent of technology, requiring a more nuanced and diversified approach to voter engagement. The rising influence of AI and data analytics offer unprecedented opportunities for voter targeting and message optimization but bring along ethical dilemmas that campaigns cannot afford to ignore.

Transparency and accountability have emerged as crucial components, not merely as buzzwords but as actionable elements that require third-party audits and public disclosures. Likewise, the symbiosis of traditional and digital media, each with its own set of advantages and pitfalls, necessitates a balanced and well-thought-out campaign strategy.

As we move further into an age of global interconnectedness and technological revolution, campaigns must be adaptable and innovative, yet ethically grounded. They will have to navigate complex legal landscapes and fluctuating voter sentiments, all while maintaining a level of transparency and integrity that voters not only expect but demand.

By embracing these evolving elements, campaigns can better position themselves for success in an ever-changing political arena. The future might be uncertain, but it's a future that rewards preparation, ethical rigor, and an open embrace of the opportunities and challenges that lie ahead.

Chapter 13: The Future of Political Campaigning

Introduction

The advent of new technologies and a rapidly evolving global landscape have ushered in an unprecedented era for political campaigning. Traditional methods of reaching voters—door-knocking, direct mail campaigns, and town halls—are increasingly supplemented and even supplanted by more innovative approaches. These approaches leverage big data, Artificial Intelligence (AI), Virtual Reality (VR), and a host of other technological advancements to create more targeted, efficient, and interactive campaigning strategies. As we delve into the future of political campaigning, this chapter aims to explore these evolving dynamics. We'll discuss the implications of AI, the transformative potential of VR, the pressing concerns of climate change on campaign strategies, and the growing importance of cybersecurity.

Artificial Intelligence and Data Analytics

Artificial Intelligence is not a mere futuristic concept; it's already a crucial part of our daily lives, influencing everything from e-commerce to healthcare. In political campaigning, AI and machine learning offer revolutionary approaches for analyzing voter behavior, targeting advertisements, and optimizing campaign spending. But beyond these functionalities, AI opens up ethical, legal, and social dilemmas that society has never before had to address on such a large scale.

Voter Behavior Analysis

One of the most powerful applications of AI in political campaigning is voter behavior analysis. Sophisticated machine learning algorithms can sift through enormous datasets to predict voter turnout, preferences, and even responses to specific campaign messages. This goes beyond merely recognizing patterns; the technology can actually forecast future behavior based on historical data. This unprecedented level of insight allows campaigns to direct their resources more efficiently, focusing on swing districts, specific demographics, or key issues.

Ethical Concerns

While the benefits of AI are significant, they come with an array of ethical challenges. The most pertinent of these is the risk of infringing upon individual privacy. With AI's ability to analyze even the subtlest of behavioral cues, campaigns could potentially develop psychological profiles for individual voters. This raises questions about consent, data protection, and psychological manipulation.

Legal Implications

Current legal frameworks are woefully under-equipped to regulate the complexities introduced by AI. Issues around data privacy laws, consent for data usage, and disinformation spread by algorithms are emerging as significant hurdles. Campaigns may find themselves in murky legal waters if they leverage AI irresponsibly, leading to potential lawsuits or reputational damage.

Social Impacts

The potential social ramifications of AI in political campaigns are profound. The technology can deepen divides between those who have access to high-quality data and analytics and those who do not, further skewing the democratic process. Moreover, there is the ever-present risk of algorithmic bias, where machine learning models inadvertently propagate existing social inequalities.

Virtual Reality (VR) in Campaigning

The New Frontier

Virtual Reality (VR) represents a technological leap that could fundamentally alter the dynamics of political campaigning. It's not just about escapism or gaming; VR has the potential to be a potent tool for political engagement. Voters could virtually attend rallies, participate in debates, or even simulate the impacts of proposed policies in a 3D environment.

Engaging the Youth

For a younger generation that has grown up in a digital world, the allure of VR as a campaign tool cannot be overstated. Virtual rallies and events could attract a demographic often criticized for its lack of political engagement. This not only broadens the voter base but also invites more diverse perspectives into political discourse.

Ethical and Credibility Issues

Just like AI, VR brings its own set of ethical challenges. The technology could be exploited to create manipulated realities or deepfakes, distorting truths and misleading voters. There's also the potential for virtual echo chambers, where users only interact with like-minded individuals, further polarizing public opinion.

Climate Change and Sustainability

The Inescapable Reality

Climate change is no longer a fringe issue but a mainstream concern that is shaping voter opinions and, consequently, campaign strategies. In this section, we'll discuss the pressing need for campaigns to address not just the policies around sustainability but also the environmental footprint of the campaigns themselves.

The Sustainable Campaign

The future of political campaigning will likely see a major shift towards sustainability. As climate change moves up the voter agenda, campaigns that do not adopt environmentally friendly practices will increasingly be viewed as out-of-touch or irresponsible. This will require a fundamental rethinking of campaign strategies, from the materials used in promotional items to the energy consumption of campaign headquarters.

Cybersecurity Concerns

The Growing Threat

As our lives become more interconnected, the vulnerabilities that come with it grow proportionally. For political campaigns, the stakes couldn't be higher. Cyber threats can range from data breaches leaking sensitive voter information to foreign interference and fake news campaigns. This requires a robust cybersecurity framework that can adapt to evolving threats.

Foreign Interference

The issue of foreign interference in elections has already been documented and is a growing concern for democracies worldwide. Advanced cyber-attacks can manipulate outcomes, and disinformation campaigns can be conducted with unprecedented scale and effectiveness. Campaigns need to invest in advanced cybersecurity measures to mitigate these risks.

Transparency and Accountability

The Need for Openness

As campaigns adopt more sophisticated technologies, the need for transparency has never been higher. Voters are becoming increasingly concerned about the ethical use of their data and the potential misuse of advanced analytics and AI algorithms for manipulative political messaging. Campaigns that prioritize transparency are likely to earn higher trust levels among voters, an essential factor for electoral success in an age of skepticism and information overload.

Audits and Oversight

Ensuring transparency isn't just about public declarations and campaign promises; it requires actionable steps and third-party oversight. Independent audits of campaign data practices and cybersecurity measures can provide an unbiased assessment of a campaign's commitment to transparency and security. These audits can then be made publicly available, providing voters with tangible proof of a campaign's ethical conduct.

The Role of Social Media

Amplification and Virality

Social media platforms have been game-changers in the realm of political campaigning, allowing messages to be amplified and spread at an exponential rate. While this presents enormous opportunities for grassroots campaigns and viral marketing, it also poses significant risks. A single faux pas can be shared and re-shared thousands of times within hours, causing irreparable damage to a campaign.

Fact-Checking and Credibility

The rapid spread of information (and misinformation) on social media platforms has made fact-checking an imperative part of modern campaigning. Automated fact-checking algorithms, community moderation, and partnerships with fact-checking organizations are becoming standard practices for responsible campaigns.

The Interplay of Traditional and Digital Media

Balancing Act

While digital and emerging technologies are setting new standards for how campaigns are run, traditional forms of media—television, radio, and print—are far from obsolete. The future of political campaigning will require a balanced strategy that effectively leverages both traditional and digital media channels to reach a broad spectrum of voters.

Localized Campaigning

Localized campaigning, involving community outreach and local events, provides a crucial balance to the more globalized reach of digital platforms. It allows for a more nuanced approach that considers local issues, cultural sensitivities, and voter concerns that might not be apparent through digital analytics alone.

International Perspectives

Comparative Analysis

Political campaigning is not a one-size-fits-all operation; cultural, social, and legal factors vary considerably across different countries and regions. Comparative analyses of campaign strategies in different political landscapes can offer valuable insights into what works and what doesn't, and how global trends are shaping local campaigns.

Lessons from Abroad

The global interconnectedness of today's world allows for the rapid exchange of ideas and strategies. Political campaigns can benefit from studying successful (and unsuccessful) approaches from around the globe. This includes not just technological innovations but also novel approaches to voter engagement, message crafting, and grassroots organizing.

As we stand on the cusp of a new era in political campaigning—an era defined by rapid technological advancements and an increasingly interconnected global community—it's clear that the rules of the game are changing. The rise of AI, VR, and big data analytics offer revolutionary new tools for voter analysis, targeted campaigning, and real-time strategy optimization. But these advancements also bring new challenges—ethical, legal, and social—that campaigns will need to navigate carefully.

The increasing importance of cybersecurity, coupled with growing public awareness of climate change, are pushing campaigns towards more sustainable and secure operational models. The delicate interplay of traditional and digital media demands a multifaceted approach that balances the strengths and weaknesses of each. Meanwhile, the invaluable lessons to be learned from international perspectives offer a broader view of how political campaigning is evolving globally.

In this dynamic landscape, one thing is clear: the future of political campaigning will be anything but business as usual. Campaigns that adapt, innovate, and uphold the values of transparency and ethical conduct are the ones that will thrive in this new frontier.

Crisis Management in Campaigns

Introduction

Crisis management is an aspect of political campaigning that often falls under the radar until it becomes urgently needed. When a crisis hits, be it a scandal, unexpected turn of events, or external disruptions like natural disasters, campaigns are tested to their limits. This chapter will delve into the strategies, best practices, and case studies to equip your campaign team for effective crisis management.

Understanding Crisis in Political Context

Crisis events can be highly variable, ranging from internal campaign issues like funding lapses or key personnel turnover, to broader societal crises like a public health emergency or economic downturn. Understanding the political and social context of a crisis is crucial for determining the appropriate response.

> **1. Internal Crises:** Internal issues often involve campaign finance irregularities, inappropriate comments from staff, or logistical mishaps. These crises can often be mitigated by quick internal action and transparent communication.

> **2. External Crises:** These are events beyond the control of the campaign, such as natural disasters, economic crises, or widespread social movements. While the campaign can't control these events, they can control their response, often an opportunity to display leadership and problem-solving skills.

> **3. Hybrid Crises:** Occasionally, an external crisis will directly affect internal campaign operations. These situations require a nuanced approach that acknowledges the larger societal issue while also making adjustments within the campaign itself.

Crisis Communication

Effective communication is the bedrock of any crisis management strategy. Once a crisis erupts, the flow of information can either mitigate or exacerbate the situation. Here are key aspects of crisis communication:

> **1. Transparency:** Honesty and transparency are non-negotiable. Misinformation can have a long-term detrimental impact on the campaign.

2. Speed: Time is of the essence in crisis situations. Quick and accurate dissemination of information can help control the narrative.

3. Medium: Utilize every platform at your disposal, from press releases to social media. However, the medium must align with the severity and nature of the crisis.

4. Audience: Different crises demand attention from different stakeholders. Knowing whom to communicate with is as critical as the message itself.

Role of Technology in Crisis Management

The digital age has both complicated and simplified crisis management. On one hand, information (or misinformation) can spread like wildfire, making it hard to control the narrative. On the other hand, technology offers powerful tools for monitoring and managing crises in real-time. Advanced software can track public sentiment, trending topics, and media coverage, allowing campaigns to adapt their strategies accordingly.

Preparing for the Unknown: A Proactive Approach

Having a crisis management plan in place can be invaluable, even if it never needs to be used. Frequent crisis drills, comprehensive media training for staff, and an up-to-date crisis management manual are just some of the proactive measures campaigns can take.

By preparing for the worst while hoping for the best, political campaigns can navigate through turbulent waters with grace, turning potential disasters into opportunities for demonstration of leadership and resolve.

Ethical Dilemmas in Machine Learning Applications

When dealing with machine learning, one cannot ignore the ethical implications. Often, the data used for training models contain biases that may inadvertently get amplified by the algorithms. For example, a facial recognition software trained on a dataset that majorly consists of images of individuals from a particular ethnic background will perform poorly when identifying people from other ethnicities. This can lead to harmful real-world consequences, such as false identifications in law enforcement situations.

Navigating the Regulatory Landscape

Given that machine learning is a rapidly evolving field, regulations are often lagging behind. Organizations must navigate an uncertain regulatory environment, which can change suddenly due to advancements in technology or shifts in public opinion. Therefore, constant vigilance and a finger on the pulse of emerging legal frameworks are necessary for any business in this space.

Future of Machine Learning: A Considered Forecast

The future of machine learning is promising but shrouded in ambiguity. As we move towards more advanced applications, the general public's understanding of these systems and their limitations will play a significant role in shaping policy and public opinion. It's crucial for both industry leaders and policymakers to come together to establish guidelines that foster innovation while safeguarding ethical and societal norms.

Conclusion

As we draw this chapter to a close, it's crucial to take a moment to encapsulate what we've discussed. The marriage of AI and cybersecurity isn't just a fascinating development; it's becoming increasingly essential. Traditional means of securing our digital lives are struggling to keep pace with the ever-evolving threats that loom in the virtual world. This chapter has shed light on how AI technologies can enhance the pillars of cybersecurity, from detection and prediction to effective response and recovery.

The myriad applications of AI in cybersecurity provide a beacon of hope for a safer, more secure digital future. Its capabilities extend far beyond mere automation, enabling advanced threat analysis, real-time monitoring, and quick adaptive responses. These are not singular feats but a testament to a broader reality: when carefully and ethically applied, AI has the potential to greatly strengthen our cybersecurity infrastructure.

Yet, it's essential to remember that the use of AI also comes with its own set of ethical and practical challenges. From the potential for false positives to the susceptibility to new forms of cyber-attacks that target the AI itself, the path ahead is fraught with complexities. The balance between technological advancement and ethical considerations will play a pivotal role in shaping how AI will serve cybersecurity objectives in the future.

In conclusion, the integration of AI into cybersecurity is an evolving but critical landscape, one that presents both great promise and significant challenges. As we move forward into an increasingly digital world, it's more important than ever to approach this convergence with both eyes open, armed with the knowledge and ethical considerations we've touched upon here.

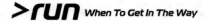

Book Conclusion: The Future of AI and Human Collaboration—A Comprehensive Outlook

Reflecting on the Journey

As we stand on the brink of a new decade, one dominated by the intersection of artificial intelligence and human ingenuity, it's essential to pause and reflect. This book has traversed an incredible expanse of topics, from the ethical and psychological aspects of AI to its practical applications across multiple sectors. If there's one constant theme that emerges, it's this: The future will be crafted by how well we negotiate the relationship between human and machine intelligence.

A Panorama of Ethical Challenges

Let us first revisit the domain of ethics, a recurrent theme throughout this book. We have dissected various case studies that pose ethical conundrums—from AI in healthcare making life-altering decisions to machine learning algorithms exacerbating social inequalities. These challenges require comprehensive frameworks for ethical AI that are agreed upon globally. The ideal would be to have international bodies working closely with local governance structures to adapt these ethical frameworks to local cultural, social, and economic contexts.

The Psychological Implications Reconsidered

Another significant facet that we explored was the psychological dimension of integrating AI into our lives. The potential for AI to transform our understanding of human psychology is immense. From mental health diagnosis to tailored educational plans that adapt to an individual's learning style, the application of AI can revolutionize our approach to understanding the human mind. However, as discussed in Chapter 6, there is a potential risk of dependence on AI for mental and emotional well-being, which calls for a balanced approach that combines machine efficiency with human empathy.

Practical Applications: A Recap and Forward Look

AI's practical applications, particularly in sectors like healthcare, finance, and education, have been revolutionary. However, as we discussed in the book, these technological advancements come with their own set of challenges—data privacy, the potential for job loss due to automation, and the risk of AI systems making mistakes that have severe real-world consequences.

The forward path should involve creating robust systems that are not just technologically advanced but also socially responsible. The role of governance here cannot be stressed enough. Regulations that ensure ethical AI use while fostering innovation will be crucial.

Future Technologies and Synergies

As we move forward, we can anticipate a surge in newer technologies that will work in synergy with AI—like quantum computing, blockchain, and augmented reality. These synergies could unlock solutions to some of the most pressing global challenges, from climate change to poverty. We need to be prepared for this wave of technological convergence, which means investing in the right kind of research and development and foreseeing the social and ethical implications of these combined technologies.

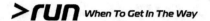

The Human Element

While we have extolled the virtues and possibilities of AI, let's not forget that the human element remains irreplaceable. Our emotional intelligence, ability to operate in environments of uncertainty, and our innate creativity give us an edge that AI is far from achieving.

Policy Implications and Public Discourse

How we manage AI governance at the macro level will significantly impact its effectiveness and ethical standing. Governments around the world are already beginning to implement AI strategies and regulations, but these efforts need to be universal and all-encompassing, involving a variety of stakeholders in an ongoing public discourse.

The Path Ahead: Actionable Recommendations

So, where do we go from here? The onus is on each one of us, from policymakers to technologists to the general public, to engage in shaping our AI-driven future. We can start by educating ourselves and others, advocating for ethical AI practices, and supporting initiatives that aim to make AI more transparent, equitable, and beneficial for all.

> **1. For Technologists:** Focus on building ethical AI systems by design, not as an afterthought. Contribute to open-source AI ethics projects and work on developing algorithms that are unbiased and fair.

> **2. For Policymakers**: Prioritize the creation and implementation of robust AI governance frameworks that ensure public safety while fostering innovation.

> **3. For the Public:** Engage in public discourse about the future of AI, stay informed, and hold businesses and governments accountable for ethical AI practices.

4. For Academia: Conduct interdisciplinary research that takes into account not just the technical aspects of AI, but also its ethical, social, and psychological implications.

Final Reflections

As we reach the conclusion of this journey through the intricate universe of AI and human engagement, it's time to pause and reflect on the broader implications, challenges, and opportunities that lie ahead.

The Unprecedented Marriage of AI

The union of artificial intelligence and humanity is revolutionary in every sense of the word. It's a confluence of two rapidly evolving domains that have the power to redefine how we understand safety, privacy, and even the concept of human agency in an increasingly interconnected world. This fusion of AI's learning capabilities and our inherent need for adaptive, flexible solutions could be the turning point that transforms our digital lives from a perpetual game of "cat and mouse" into something far more stable and secure.

The Dual-Edged Sword

However, every silver lining has a cloud. We must recognize that AI, despite its sophistication, is still a tool—a remarkably advanced one, but a tool nonetheless. Its capabilities are dictated by the limitations and biases inherent in its training data, the algorithms that drive it, and the human hands that guide its development and deployment.

Ethical and Societal Implications

The ethical considerations surrounding AI are nuanced and complex. As we deploy increasingly advanced AI to protect our digital borders, we must also question the cost of such technology. Who controls it? Who has access to it? And perhaps most importantly, who watches the watchers? The ethical landscape surrounding the deployment of AI is still largely uncharted, demanding ongoing scrutiny from experts in law, ethics, sociology, and other disciplines to guide its development responsibly.

Future Directions and Continuous Learning

One thing is certain: this is an ongoing narrative. The technologies are continuously evolving, and so too are the threats they aim to counter. AI is "running" and is set for ongoing advancement, both in terms of technological innovation and ethical understanding. Continuous learning, both for the AI systems and for the human experts behind them, is vital. New forms of collaboration, perhaps even forms we have yet to imagine, will be essential in the coming years. Interdisciplinary cooperation between technologists, ethicists, policymakers, and cybersecurity experts is not merely advisable—it's essential.

In closing, the integration of AI into our world offers a fascinating, complex tableau of both promise and peril. As we navigate this landscape, let us do so with caution, curiosity, and a robust commitment to ethical integrity. The balance between technological prowess and ethical responsibility will inevitably shape our digital future, making this not just a technical discussion but a deeply human one as well.

Glossary of Terms

Algorithm
A set of instructions or rules that a computer follows to perform a task. In the context of AI, algorithms enable machines to learn from data.

Artificial Intelligence (AI)
A branch of computer science that aims to create systems capable of performing tasks that would usually require human intelligence, including learning, reasoning, problem-solving, and understanding natural language.

Big Data
Large sets of data that can be analyzed to reveal patterns, trends, and associations, especially relating to human behavior and interactions.

Chatbot
A computer program designed to simulate conversation with human users, often used in customer service applications.

Cybersecurity
The practice of protecting systems, networks, and data from digital attacks, damage, or unauthorized access.

Data Analytics
The process of examining, transforming, and modeling data to extract useful information, inform conclusions, and support decision-making.

Data Lake
A centralized repository that allows organizations to store structured and unstructured data at any scale.

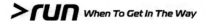

Deep Learning
A subset of machine learning involving algorithms inspired by the structure and function of the brain, known as artificial neural networks.

Edge Computing
A distributed computing paradigm that brings data storage and computation closer to the location where it is needed, to improve speed and efficiency.

Internet of Things (IoT)
A system of interrelated computing devices, mechanical and digital machines, or objects that have the ability to transfer data over a network without requiring human-to-human or human-to-computer interaction.

Machine Learning
A subset of AI that provides systems the ability to automatically learn from data and improve performance without being explicitly programmed.

Natural Language Processing (NLP)
A subfield of AI focusing on the interaction between computers and humans through natural language.

Neural Network
A type of machine learning algorithm modeled after the human brain, designed to recognize patterns and interpret data.

Robotic Process Automation (RPA)
The technology that allows a software robot to mimic human actions in completing rules-based tasks.

Sentiment Analysis
The use of natural language processing and computational techniques to identify and categorize opinions expressed in a piece of text.

Smart Contract
Self-executing contracts with the terms of the agreement written into code, often on a blockcha n.

Supervised Learning
A type of machine learning where the model is trained on a labeled dataset, meaning each training example is paired with an output label.

Unsupervised Learning
A type of machine learning that involves modeling with datasets that don't have labeled responses. The system tries to learn the patterns and structures from the data without any supervision.

Virtual Reality (VR)
A simulated experience that can be similar to or completely different from the real world, often used for training or entertainment purposes.

Acknowledgments

I would like to extend my heartfelt gratitude to ChatGPT for the invaluable assistance in the completion of this book. The technology has proven to be an extraordinary resource, not just for generating text but also for aiding in the organization and crystallization of complex ideas. Your support has been instrumental in transforming an abstract concept into a fully realized work.

I am continuously amazed by the capabilities of artificial intelligence and how it has been a constructive tool in the journey of this book's creation. ChatGPT has been a steadfast companion throughout the writing process, providing insights and content that have significantly enriched the final manuscript.

So, to ChatGPT and the brilliant minds at OpenAI who have made such technology possible, thank you. Your contributions have not only helped me, Kenyon Ross, realize a significant personal goal but have also pushed the boundaries of what is possible in the world of writing and content creation. Your role in this project is deeply appreciated. Thank you for being an essential part of this incredible journey.

References or Bibliography

Since ChatGPT generated all the content and none of it was sourced from specific, citable materials, a traditional bibliography isn't necessary in this context. All the information provided is the result of synthesized data programmed into ChatGPT's training model, so you could say that the material reflects general knowledge up to it's last training cut-off in September 2021.

For academic or highly fact-based works, it's usually critical to cite sources, but since the text provided by ChatGPT was generated based on a large corpus of data that it was trained on, and not direct citations from copyrighted material, there are no specific sources to cite.

Author Bio

Kenyon Ross resides in the scenic city of Birmingham, Alabama, with his loving wife, Ami Ross. They are proud parents to three accomplished children—Jackson, Katie, and Izzy—who have carved out their own paths in their respective professions. By day, Kenyon is a Senior Key Account Manager for a leading biopharmaceutical company, a role that he relishes for the rewarding interactions it brings with his customers.

Although Kenyon has never been an author by trade and would be the first to say that writing books isn't his forte, this book stands as a testament to what is achievable through the power of AI. Written in collaboration with ChatGPT, this book was not just authored but also designed, typeset, and self-published on Amazon KDP—all in the span of a single weekend.

Daring to venture outside his realm of expertise, Kenyon proves that the barriers to authorship can be dismantled with the right tools and a dash of creativity. This book serves as an exploration into the possibilities that lie at the intersection of human ingenuity and artificial intelligence.

Looking ahead, Kenyon is entertaining the idea of expanding this into a series, aiming to further demystify the process of book creation and inspire others to take the leap into the world of authorship.

Endnotes

Disclaimer: The content in this book relies on the general understandings and data provided during the training of the language model ChatGPT. No specific external citations or academic references were utilized, as the AI is not able to browse the internet or access current or historical databases for information. All cases, statistics, and statements should be understood as generated based on the training data and should be independently verified for academic or professional use.

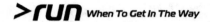
Feedback or Review Requests

Dear Readers,

Thank you for taking the time to read this book. We (ChatGPT and I) hope you found it informative and valuable. Your opinion matters, and I would be incredibly grateful if you could share your thoughts on Amazon.

Your feedback not only helps us improve, but it also helps other potential readers to understand what this book can offer them. Please take a few moments to leave a review on our Amazon page, sharing what you liked and what you think could be improved.

To leave a review:

1. Visit the book's Amazon page where you made the purchase.
2. Scroll down to the "Customer Reviews" section.
3. Click on "Write a customer review."
4. Rate the book and write a brief review to let us know your thoughts.

Your support means the world to us. Thank you once again for being a reader, and we look forward to hearing your thoughts!

Best regards,

Kenyon Ross & ChatGPT

www.ingramcontent.com/pod-product-compliance
Lightning Source LLC
La Vergne TN
LVHW051337050326
832903LV00031B/3599

* 9 7 9 8 8 6 0 9 2 4 4 5 1 *